Praise for *Ma*

"Marriage God's Way is a thorough and comprehensive treatment of marriage. The reader who works his way through this volume will be richly rewarded."

> **Tedd Tripp**—Husband of forty-eight years, pastor, speaker, and author of *Shepherding a Child's Heart*

"Most Christian books on marriage today don't have much Scripture in them. Not this one. It is saturated with the Word of God. If you want a book that is built on the foundation of exposition of Scripture, this book is for you. While Scott offers many practical insights, they are all grounded in the biblical text using biblical language. *Marriage God's Way* will fill your mind with the pure and perfect Word of God. This is what every marriage needs."

> **Scott T. Brown**—Husband of thirty-one years, director of the National Center for Family-Integrated Churches, pastor, speaker, and author of *A Theology of the Family*

"With the divorce rate for believers lagging just behind that of unbelievers, there is no shortage of Christian books on marriage. Unfortunately, few of these books offer lasting effectiveness, because they lack the authority and wisdom of Scripture. Most merely weave together tidbits of human wisdom and pop ideas spiced up with random verses. Pastor Scott understands that strong marriages need more than tidbits of wisdom and pop ideas. He knows that as the Designer of marriage, God gave us His Word as an owner's manual. Therefore, in *Marriage God's Way*, Scott draws upon the authority and wisdom of the Bible to help every couple find the passion, intimacy, and romance that God intended."

> **Reb Bradley**—Husband of thirty-eight years, pastor, speaker, founder of Family Ministries, and author of *Child Training Tips*

"*Marriage God's Way* is a book that will greatly bless your marriage. Pastor Scott combines personal experience, pastoral care, and above all, clear teaching from Scripture to guide his readers into a proper understanding of what God intends for their marriage. In a world where marriage is often considered a hopeless attempt at fleeting happiness, a book like this will give the Christian couple biblical perspective, good counsel, and hope for their future together. If you are looking for help to restore your struggling marriage, or you just need a good reminder of why godly marriages work, this book provides sound guidance, and I highly recommend it to you."

David Eddy—Husband of twenty-five years and pastor

"Scott LaPierre has clearly gone on a mining expedition through the Scriptures and unearthed some wonderful hidden treasures from God's Word. He writes in an easy to read, relatable style, which left me always ready to jump into the next chapter. Every page is filled with simple truths that often become neglected in our conflict-filled, sex-saturated, self-centered culture. *Marriage God's Way* is a precious gem. Meticulous. Practical. Packed with valuable pearls while being culturally significant. This book touches every aspect of what it is to both love and respect each other as your marriage prospers. Read it!"

John Leffler, D.Min.—Husband of thirty-three years and pastor

"Scott beautifully expounds upon the best, and ultimately the only way to do marriage—God's way. If you want to have a successful, thriving marriage, read and apply what is in this book."

Joshua Zarzana—Husband of thirteen years, family pastor, and author of *The Son Who Chases the Father*

"*Marriage God's Way* captures the heart of a profoundly needed biblical perspective for marriages everywhere. This is a must read for anyone who desires to embrace and reflect the beauty of Christ in their relationship."

James Lindstrand—Husband of seventeen years, pastor, and author of *Porn, Purity and Pickles*

"*Marriage God's Way* is an honest look at the beautiful institution of marriage through the eyes of Scott LaPierre, a husband, father, and pastor. He takes time to thoroughly cover the distinct roles and building blocks of marriage, carefully relating the principles of Scripture as they apply to each facet. Through personal illustrations and skillful exegesis of the Word, he brings refreshing insight to the heartaches, struggles, and joys that commonly accompany relationships. You will find sage advice, biblical insights, and heartwarming perspective as you read each chapter. Definitely a worthy book for the newlywed or the marriage veteran!"

> **Dale and Lisa Jost**—Married for thirty-five years, parents and managers of *The Josties*

"It is well-known that Christian marriages look like and last as long as their non-Christian counterparts. This sends the message that Jesus Christ is impotent to save Christian marriages or that Christians disregard the Bible's instructions for marriage. This is where Pastor Scott's succinct book comes in, as he places the responsibility squarely on the shoulders of Christians. As a young pastor, it did not take long for Scott to discover one of the greatest challenges facing Christians: building a healthy and joyful marriage that honors Christ. *Marriage God's Way* is serious reading, meant to cut through the fluff and deliver hard-hitting biblical commentary designed to set the record straight. Because of the terse content, the book would be ideal for Christian teens, young adults preparing for ministry, and of course, couples of all kinds. "

> **Dr. Terry O'Hare**—Husband of thirty-six years and author of *The Sabbath Complete*

"*Marriage God's Way* is a thorough, biblical, and engaging study of God's truth regarding marriage. It covers a wide range of areas in a transparent, clear, and relevant manner that both brings light to the text and provides the specifics in order to live out God's truth in our marriages so that He is glorified."

> **Joe Gruchacz**—Husband of thirty-two years and pastor

MARRIAGE GOD'S WAY

A Biblical Recipe for Healthy, Joyful, Christ-Centered Relationships

Scott LaPierre

www.ScottLaPierre.org | scott@scottlapierre.org

ISBN: 0692689354
ISBN 13: 978-0692689356
Library of Congress Control Number: 2016904997
Charis Family Publishing

Unless otherwise indicated all Scripture quotations are taken from the New King James Version®. Copyright © 1982 by Thomas Nelson. Used by permission. All rights reserved. Abbreviations used for other versions:

- AMP—Scripture quotations taken from the Amplified® Bible, Copyright © 2015 by The Lockman Foundation. Used by permission.
- ESV—The ESV® Bible (The Holy Bible, English Standard Version®) copyright © 2001 by Crossway, a publishing ministry of Good News Publishers. ESV® Text Edition: 2011. The ESV® text has been reproduced in cooperation with and by permission of Good News Publishers. All rights reserved.
- NASB—Scripture taken from the NEW AMERICAN STANDARD BIBLE®, Copyright © 1960, 1962, 1963, 1968, 1971, 1972, 1973, 1975, 1977, 1995 by The Lockman Foundation. Used by permission.
- NIV—THE HOLY BIBLE, NEW INTERNATIONAL VERSION®, NIV® Copyright © 1973, 1978, 1984, 2011 by Biblica, Inc.® Used by permission. All rights reserved worldwide.

With the exception of the Amplified Bible, Scripture quotations with brackets, parentheses, or italics are the emphasis of the author.

Dedication

Marriage God's Way is dedicated to my father, John LaPierre.

Dear Dad,

Thank you for showing me what it looks like to be a loving, dedicated husband and a strong spiritual leader. Thank you for your love and commitment to Katie, our children, and me. Thank you for the way you have courageously handled the trials you've faced.

After I became a Christian, my greatest desire was for you and Mom to come to know Christ as well. That I would be privileged enough to baptize the two of you and have you serve as a deacon at the church I pastor has shown me that God indeed "is able to do exceedingly abundantly above all that we ask or think" (Ephesians 3:20).

To see how the gospel transformed you has strengthened my faith and been one of the greatest joys of my life. You are a humble, gentle servant, and I would feel blessed to be more like you.

I love you so much.

Your son,
Scott

Acknowledgments

First, I want to thank the wonderful congregation at Woodland Christian Church. Your hunger for Scripture encourages me in my study each week. There are few blessings greater for a pastor than knowing he can stand behind the pulpit and boldly proclaim God's Word to saints who love the truth.

Second, I want to thank Kandie Schmitz, Pastor Doug Connell, David Devine, Lauren Cash, and Dr. Terrence O'Hare for proofreading *Marriage God's Way*. Your thoughts and suggestions were invaluable.

Third, I could not ask for a more wonderful woman to have by my side through this life. Katie, thank you for all the ways you help me, including being a wife who makes it easier to obey God's commands for husbands. You have all of my heart, and I am more in love with you now than I have ever been.

Finally, I want to thank my Lord and Savior, Jesus Christ, the true and greater subject of this book. Every husband should strive to be to his bride what Christ is to the church, and every wife should strive to be to her husband what the church should be to Christ.

Table of Contents

Introduction xiii

Part I: *Recognize That . . .* 1

Your Marriage Reflects Your Relationship with Christ 1

Marriage "Problems" Are Really Symptoms 9

Part II: Genesis 1–3 *Creation of Marriage and the Fall* 17

God's Establishment of Adam's Headship 18

Male Leadership Is God's Pattern 27

The Help a Man Needs 37

Consequences of the Fall for Husbands and Wives 49

Part III: *Understanding Love* 61

What Is Love? 63

Characteristics of *Agape* 71

Part IV: Ephesians 5:25–33 *A Husband's Call to Agape and a Wife's Call to Respect* 79

A Husband Should *Agape* His Wife 81

Protecting the Sanctity of Marriage 93

A Wife Should Respect Her Husband 103

Part V: *Understanding Submission* 115

Equal Opportunity Submission 117

What Submission Does Not Mean 129

Putting Your Husband in a Position to Lead 139

Part VI: 1 Peter 3:1–7 *A Wife's Beauty and a Husband's Treatment* 149

    Winning Over Your Husband...151

    A Woman's Greater Beauty 163

    The Bible's "Perfect" Wife..173

    A Husband Treats His Wife Well By 183

Part VII: I Corinthians 7:1–6 *A Biblical View of Intimacy*...........193

    The Case for Intimacy 195

    When Intimacy Is Threatened.......................................203

Part VIII: Matthew 7:24–27 *A Strong Foundation*.......................209

    Building on Christ..211

    The Importance of Obeying 215

    Epilogue: The Mystery of Marriage...............................219

Introduction

There are thousands of marriage books, so why another one? What makes this one different? Is there any reason you should trust me to write it?

First, and of greatest importance, I am not asking you to trust me. This book is not a collection of my thoughts about marriage. Rather, I am inviting you to trust God because He is the author of marriage. He designed the roles and responsibilities for husbands and wives. He knows what a couple needs to have a healthy, joyful, Christ-centered relationship, and He provided a recipe for that in His Word. My desire is to present that recipe clearly and biblically in *Marriage God's Way*.

Second, I wrote this book because I am passionate about this area of Scripture and life. God designed the family as the primary unit for every other segment in society, including the church. And marriage is the heart of the family. As a marriage disintegrates, the family disintegrates. As families disintegrate, churches disintegrate. As churches disintegrate, society disintegrates.

When marriages are strong, however, families are strong. When families are strong, churches can be strong because strong churches are made up of strong families. As a pastor, I have seen many struggling marriages, but I have also seen couples find the solutions to their problems in Scripture. The truth of God's Word has the power to heal and strengthen any marriage.

Third, because the marriage relationship is a picture of Christ and His relationship to the church, it is one of the greatest evangelistic tools believers have. Godly marriages have the potential to reveal Christ to an unbelieving world. That alone is a reason I am passionate about seeing marriages strengthened.

Finally, I wrote *Marriage God's Way* because as a husband I have experienced firsthand the blessings that come from obeying God's Word and the negative consequences that come with disobedience. My wife, Katie, and I grew up in the same small town (McArthur, California) and went to school together. We both became Christians in our twenties, and soon after were married.

At times the stresses of being a husband, a father, and a senior pastor (a role that alone could keep me busy from the moment I get up to the moment I go to bed) have put a huge amount of pressure on our marriage. In the following chapters, I will share some of our personal struggles. When I ask you to trust that God's Word provides a recipe for healthy, joyful marriages, I do so because I have experienced this truth in my relationship with Katie.

Part I:

Recognize That . . .

Chapter One

Your Marriage Reflects Your Relationship with Christ

A few years ago, Katie and I faced the biggest crisis of our marriage. I started pastoring Woodland Christian Church when it was fairly small, but within three years the congregation had tripled in size. I admit that before I became a pastor, I was completely unaware of how much work is actually involved in shepherding a church of even a few hundred people. I had been an Army officer, a supervisor at a distribution center for Target, and an elementary school teacher. But none of those occupations approached the amount of mental and emotional energy and sheer hard work pastoring entails!

Almost all of my waking hours were packed with studying, teaching, counseling, making phone calls, sending e-mails, attending meetings, addressing administrative responsibilities, and tending to benevolence issues. When I was home, where I should have been an engaged father and husband, I did not have much left for my family emotionally, mentally, or physically.

Although I was failing as a husband and father, I was able to convince myself I was still pleasing the Lord. I compartmentalized my life by saying, "I am a Christian first. I am a spouse second. I am a parent third. I am an employee fourth." Instead, I should have said, "I am a Christian spouse. I am a Christian parent. I am a Christian employee." The danger of seeing ourselves as a Christian first and a spouse second is we can find ourselves believing the lie I bought into at the time: "If I can be a good pastor, I can please God even though I am not the best husband." The truth is that I was a poor husband, and I should have recognized that meant I was *not* pleasing the Lord.

The reason we cannot please the Lord while failing as a husband or wife is that our Christianity is directly related to the way we treat our spouses. Our marriages are an outpouring of our relationship with Christ:

- In Matthew 7:16b, Jesus asked: "Do men gather grapes from thornbushes or figs from thistles?"
- In James 3:12, the apostle James asked: "Does a spring send forth fresh water and bitter from the same opening? Can a fig tree, my brethren, bear olives, or a grapevine bear figs?"

The point of these verses is that we reveal our Christianity by the way we live. As Jesus clarified: "You will know them by their fruits" (Matthew 7:16a).

Since our relationships with our spouses are our most important earthly relationship, what we are as spouses is a reflection of what we are as Christians. Later, we will discuss the marriage passage in Ephesians 5:21–33, but for now it is worth mentioning two commands that give us the standard for marriage:

- Ephesians 5:25—Husbands, love your wives, just as Christ also loved the church and gave Himself for her.
- Ephesians 5:22—Wives, submit to your own husbands, as to the Lord.[1]

Since the Lord gave us these commands, our obedience to them reflects our relationship with Christ. This is why there is no such thing as

---

[1] Chapter 13 addresses the "what-ifs" of submission: "What about an abusive husband? When does a wife not need to submit?"

a spiritually mature man who does not love his wife nor a spiritually mature woman who does not submit to her husband:

- A husband cannot love Christ without loving his wife.
- A wife cannot submit to Christ without submitting to her husband.

A husband is to love and cherish his wife not because she is perfect, or because she treats him the way he wants to be treated. A husband loves and cherishes his wife because he loves Christ. Likewise, a wife submits to her husband not because he is a wonderful spiritual leader, or because he loves her the way she wants to be loved. A wife submits to her husband because she wants to submit to Christ.

A husband's love and a wife's submission is not a test of their obedience to their spouses. It is a test of their obedience to the Lord. This might sound discouraging, but it should actually be encouraging. When a husband knows his love and a wife knows her submission is an act of obedience to Christ, it can be that much easier. There will be times when a husband does not want to love his wife and a wife does not want to submit to her husband. In those moments husbands and wives can tell themselves: "I am doing this out of my love for Christ. I am submitting to the Lord, because of what He has done for me."

I would never try to convince a husband that his wife is worthy of his love, or try to convince a wife that her husband is worthy of her submission. The fact is, their spouses are not. But Christ is worthy of a husband's love and a wife's submission. It is important to understand this principle before we examine God's instructions for husbands and wives because this will give us the necessary motivation to obey.

The obvious questions, then, are: How can a husband love his wife just as Christ loved the church? How can a wife submit to her husband as unto the Lord?

Trust the Holy Spirit to Help You

Unfortunately, when it comes to our marriages we often feel alone. God's standard for husbands and wives is so high that we ask, "Who is going to help me obey these commands?"

Two words that summarize what it is like thinking about being the husbands and wives God commands us to be are "intimidating" and "overwhelming." As a husband, it is intimidating to think of being to your wife what Christ is to the church. If you are not intimidated by it, you do not understand what is expected of you. As a wife, it is overwhelming to think of submitting to your husband as you should to the Lord. If we had to obey God's commands on our own, we should feel not only overwhelmed or intimidated but completely hopeless. Because of a promise Jesus made us, though, we can feel hopeful.

Jesus told His disciples, "I will pray the Father, and He will give you another Helper, that He may abide with you forever" (John 14:16). If you have embraced the gospel, then the Holy Spirit lives in you. You are not alone! The Holy Spirit will empower you to do what God has commanded you to do.

The first half of Ephesians 5 is about living in the Spirit, and the second half is about marriage. This is fitting because if there is any area of the Christian life in which the Holy Spirit's help is necessary, it is marriage. In Ephesians 5:18, the apostle Paul states, "Do not be drunk with wine, in which is dissipation; but be filled with the Spirit." It might sound odd to compare drunkenness with being filled with the Spirit, but we can sum up Paul's point with the word "influence." People who are driving drunk are "driving under the influence." Just as alcohol has the potential to influence, so does the Holy Spirit.

The Greek word for "be filled" is *pleroo,* which means "keep on being filled" or "stay filled" with the Spirit. Paul is talking about something that should be ongoing in the lives of believers. Christians need to allow—and trust—the Holy Spirit to influence them as husbands and wives. The following verses are promises from God's Word. As you read them, consider how they apply to marriage:

- 2 Corinthians 9:8—God is able to make all grace abound toward you, that you, always having all sufficiency in all things, may have an abundance for every good work.
- Philippians 2:13—It is God who works in you both to will and to do for His good pleasure.
- Ephesians 1:19–20—The exceeding greatness of His power toward us who believe, according to the working of His mighty power which He worked in Christ when He raised Him from the dead.
- Hebrews 13:20–21—May the God of peace who brought up our Lord Jesus from the dead make you complete in every good work to do His will, working in you what is well pleasing in His sight, through Jesus Christ.

God gives us what we need to obey His commands. He is the One working in and through us to accomplish every good work. He makes this possible through the incomparably great power that raised Jesus from the dead. God wants us to be equipped to do what He has called us to do, and of all God wants from us, what could be more important than our relationships with our spouses?

Marriage is a reflection of Christ and the church. Does God want Christ and the church to have a great relationship? Absolutely! Does God want the world to witness Christian marriages that wonderfully represent Christ's relationship with the church? Without a doubt! God has given us His indwelling Spirit to help make that happen.

When we become discouraged in our marriages, these are the truths that we need to remember. It is as if God has said, "The standard I have set for husbands and wives is high, but you do not have to do this alone. I would not command you to do something without also giving you what is necessary to obey."

We Cannot Just Sit Back

Let's bring some balance to this discussion by understanding the word "help." "I will help you" is very different from "I will do everything." The Holy Spirit helps us, but we need to remember that He does not do it all for us. We still have responsibilities. The Holy Spirit is not going to supernaturally take control of a marriage when the individuals involved are not committed to putting forth the necessary effort.

The apostle Paul reveals the relationship in Ephesians 2:10: "We are His workmanship, created in Christ Jesus for good works, which God prepared beforehand that we should walk in them." God prepared good works for us, but we have to "walk in them." We do not want to miss out on what God wants to do in our marriage because we are being lazy or selfish. Consider the responsibilities placed on our shoulders elsewhere in the New Testament:

- Romans 13:13–14—Let us *walk properly* . . . *Put on* the Lord Jesus Christ, and *make no provision* for the flesh, to fulfill its lusts.
- Colossians 3:12–14—*Put on* tender mercies, kindness, humility, meekness, longsuffering; *[bear] with* one another, and *[forgive]* one another . . . *Put on* love, which is the bond of perfection.

Note the calling we are given: walk, put on, make no provision for, bear with, and forgive. What does this look like in practical terms? How does the Holy Spirit's help work with our free will? Here are some examples. We have a choice

Husband, you normally plop yourself down on the couch next to your wife, but the Holy Spirit has been compelling you to be more affectionate. So the next time you sit next to your wife, you put your arm around her. The Holy Spirit has also been leading you to be a better listener. Instead of simply hearing your wife speak, this time you nod and verbally affirm what she says. Perhaps even paraphrase her words to validate her sentiments. Since she is not used to this, your wife will notice and appreciate the extra effort.

Wife, you are riding in the car with your husband when you notice the low fuel light come on. Normally you point this out and "remind" him until he pulls into a gas station. Though he does not like this, you think it beats running out of gas. Lately, however, the Holy Spirit has been directing you to trust your husband, so this time you simply mention it and let it go. He pulls into a station, and since you have had a habit of telling him what to do, he notices the difference and is pleasantly surprised. Maybe at the pump he even says, "Thank you for not repeatedly telling me to pull over!"

In each case, the spouse would do well to verbalize his or her appreciation for the changed behavior.

These are only simple examples of how the Holy Spirit works with us. As you continue through this book, look for other ways. Be submissive and receptive to His guidance. Consider this encouraging verse that ties these thoughts together: "To this end I labor, according to [God's] working which works mightily in me" (Colossians 1:29).

The apostle Paul was discussing working side by side with God to accomplish His work. Similarly, we should see ourselves working side by side with God in our marriages. Yes, we labor to be the husbands and wives He wants us to be. But what an encouragement that while we are laboring, He also "works mightily in" us.

Chapter Two

Marriage "Problems" Are Really Symptoms

Because our relationships with our spouses are a reflection of our relationship with Christ, our marriage "problems" are really only symptoms. (The actual problems are in our relationship with Christ.) In my own marriage, for instance, the "problem" looked like I did not have enough time for my wife and children, but that was only a symptom. The problem was that I would not listen to the Holy Spirit's prompt to meet my family's needs, and I was not trusting Christ enough but instead letting anxiety consume me.

Christ Not Husband

This is why any biblical marriage counseling must address the couple's relationship with the Lord. Couples I counsel are often confused when they share a problem they are experiencing and I respond by asking, "So what does your time in God's Word look like? How is your prayer life? What about your involvement in the church?" A wife will say, "I just told you my husband yells at me. Why are you talking about his time in the Word?" Because the hope is that as a husband reads God's Word he will become convicted of his sin and repent. He will become a more patient and loving man. I do not have the power to change a husband's heart (and apparently neither does a wife or there would be no need for counseling). A husband can only become a new man through a relationship with Christ.

Likewise, a husband will respond, "I just told you how my wife humiliates me in front of our friends. Why would you mention joining a small group?" Because other believers can provide accountability, vulnerability, and transparency; you can learn from others and be challenged by their examples. When you are not involved in the body of Christ, you will not receive the encouragement and exhortation God wants you to have. You will feel alone, as though you are the only couple having these problems. You will not have anyone in your life through whom God can regularly speak to you. We are made to have fellowship with other believers, and when we do not have it, that lack manifests itself in other areas, including our marriages.

Here are two situations I have witnessed many times. A husband and wife are having marriage problems. They submit to Christ, and soon their marriage improves. Why? Did their difficulties simply disappear? No, those difficulties had been symptoms of the real problem—Christ was not supreme in their lives. When they put Christ first, their marriage improved.

Similarly, I have seen a couple plugged into church. The husband and wife pray and read the Word together. They are doing well spiritually, and their marriage is healthy. Then, for various reasons, they get distracted from the Lord and their priorities shift. They start wavering in church attendance and spiritual disciplines. They fall out of fellowship. Soon their marriage suffers.

So remember: Marriage "problems" are really only symptoms—or negative consequences—of not having Christ as the focal point in the marital relationship. If couples want a strong, healthy marriage, they need a strong, healthy relationship with Christ. When a couple's relationship with Christ is weak and unhealthy, the marriage will be weak and unhealthy.

Handling Frustrations

Marriage God's Way is not split into one section for husbands and another for wives. The biblical passages on marriage, such as Ephesians 5 and 1 Peter 3, contain intertwined exhortations for both spouses. Husbands should read the instruction for wives, and wives should read the instruction for husbands so they can understand what is commanded of their spouses. If a husband knows what is expected of his wife, and a wife knows what is expected of her husband, they can help each other fulfill their biblical responsibilities.

Although, there is also a danger associated with this approach. Since the standard set by God's Word is so high:

- A husband could easily become frustrated that his wife is not more respectful or submissive as God's Word commands.
- A wife could as easily become frustrated that her husband does not cherish her or provide the spiritual leadership God's Word commands.

This is illustrated by a situation that took place years ago when I was teaching on marriage. A woman stood up and began criticizing her husband in front of everyone. I could have interrupted and said, "Can we all just pray for you two?" or "Why don't we talk about this after the study?" Instead, I was caught so off guard that I did the worst thing possible—nothing! I simply stood there with my jaw dropped while the angry wife finished berating her husband.

After that, I decided that whenever I taught on marriage, I would remind people that the goal is to improve marriages, not to arm couples for World War III. So here are three encouragements for handling any frustrations:

1. We all have plenty of weaknesses that need to be addressed. Instead of keeping a mental account of all that your spouse does wrong, remind yourself of your own struggles.
2. Ask yourself: "How can I encourage my spouse to fulfill the role God has given him or her? Is there anything I can do that will make being married to me easier?" If you cannot think of any answers to these questions, you are not thinking hard enough.

3. Whenever you start to become frustrated toward your spouse, turn any frustrations into prayer. Take any feelings of hurt, betrayal, or disappointment, and pray that God will help your spouse grow in the area that is upsetting you. Pray also for God to help you be as forgiving and gracious as necessary. When it comes to our spouses, most people—myself included—are far more likely to complain, gossip, yell, threaten, pout, or ignore than to pray. If we would spend as much time praying for our spouses as we do on these other things, our marriages would be much better.

Embrace the Struggle

As you work through this book, recognize the tension created in your marriage is a good thing. God is introducing areas that need to be improved, and the best way to do that is by asking each other tough questions. A husband might say, "Outside of the Lord Himself, do you feel like you are taking second place to anything in my life?" If a wife answers that she does not feel she is the supreme relationship in her husband's life, the husband should not try to talk her out of the way she feels or persuade her to see things differently. Likewise, a wife might ask her husband, "Do you feel like I respect you?" If the husband explains how she makes him feel disrespected, the wife should not argue with her husband and try to convince him he is wrong. Instead, each spouse should listen to the other and try to make the appropriate changes.

When couples ask each other these difficult questions, they should expect some painful discussions. That's great. Let me give you an analogy. A few months ago, I hurt my lower back. It is a recurring injury that reminds me I am getting older. So I returned to the chiropractor. If you have ever been to a chiropractor, you know they can be pretty forceful—pushing, twisting, snapping, and popping. Sometimes you are left feeling sore, but that is supposed to happen. That is how the chiropractor makes adjustments and straightens things out.

But what if you went to the chiropractor and all he did was rub your shoulders, pat your back, and tell you everything looked fine? After that, he sat next to you and asked how your day was going. How would you react? I know how I would react: "This is not why I came here. I know if you are going to help me, you are going to have to apply some pressure and do some pushing and pulling. There is going to be some tension. There will even be a little soreness afterward." *be uncomfortable w/ Growth?*

Likewise, if we are <u>going to improve our marriage</u>s, there is going to be some <u>discomfort</u>. There is going to be some struggle and tension. We should not be alarmed, because this is part of the natural healing and strengthening process as God works in our hearts. And what is the alternative? Simple. Close this book. Be lazy. Do not ask each other the tough questions or talk about the tough issues. Do not take your marriage seriously. Do not improve as a husband, a wife, or a Christian.

If you avoid discussing the biblical teachings in this book with your spouse, you will not have any tough issues with which to wrestle. But you will not grow either, and your marriage will not be strengthened. Even if you avoid the difficult discussions and the discomfort that accompanies them now, you will more than likely experience even tougher, more uncomfortable situations later.

So I want to encourage you to embrace the struggles because of what they are going to produce. The apostle Paul tells us: "We glory in tribulations, knowing that tribulation produces perseverance; and perseverance, character, and character, hope" (Romans 5:3–4). Glory in the struggles you are having, knowing that they are producing something good as you, your spouse, and your marriage are refined!

God's Chastening Is Not Punishment, but a Father's Loving Discipline

Hebrews 12:5–6 discusses the way God produces good in our lives:

> And you have forgotten the exhortation which speaks to you as to sons: "My son, do not despise the chastening of the LORD, nor be <u>discouraged</u> when you are <u>rebuked</u> by Him; for whom the LORD loves He chastens, and scourges every son whom He receives."

13

We often apply these verses to God's punishment of sin, but the real context is God working out certain issues to produce fruit and righteousness in our lives. Since none of us is a perfect husband or wife, we all have sin in our marriages. That means each of us has certain behaviors and struggles God needs to fix as we grow in our sanctification and become more like Christ. God will chasten us to make that happen. While that does not always feel good, we should embrace the chastening, understanding that God is doing something good and worthwhile in our life.

The author of Hebrews goes on to say in verses 11–13:

> Now no chastening seems to be joyful for the present, but painful; nevertheless, afterward it yields the peaceable fruit of righteousness to those who have been trained by it. Therefore strengthen the hands which hang down, and the feeble knees, and make straight paths for your feet, so that what is lame may not be dislocated, but rather be healed.

How true are these verses! Nice, gentle back rubs feel good. They are enjoyable. But they do not do much for our lower back problems. If we really want solutions, we must experience some discomfort. Likewise, it is not easy or enjoyable to deal with our weaknesses. People do not want to talk about their struggles as a husband or wife. But that is how we grow, and that is how we allow God to work. Indeed, that is how "the peaceable fruit of righteousness" is produced in our lives.

Interestingly, the above passage suggests that this does not happen for everyone. Only certain people receive the "peaceable fruit of righteousness." According to verse 11, it is those who "have been trained by [the chastening]." The Greek word for "trained" is *gymnazo*, related to our word "gymnasium." It means to exercise vigorously. Improving our marriages is hard work. As we embrace the struggles in marriage, talking about them and working through them, we need to give ourselves the exhortation the author of Hebrews gives his readers. Let's strengthen our weak hands and feet, trusting God to make straight paths for our marriages to be healed.

As I look back at that painful time in our marriage that I discussed in the previous chapter, I am very thankful for it. Like all trials, God used it for our benefit. James 1:2–4 says:

> My brethren, count it all joy when you fall into various trials, knowing that the testing of your faith produces patience. But let patience have its perfect work, that you may be perfect and complete, lacking nothing.

One of the greatest blessings from this trial in our lives—one of the ways God used it powerfully—relates to what He taught Katie and me through it. It is not easy to understand how powerful God's Word is when you have not seen it work. It is not easy to understand the importance of obeying Scripture until you have disobeyed it and personally experienced the negative consequences.

That difficult season in my marriage taught me a number of the principles I share in this book. This is when I learned how important it is to apply God's Word and lean on the Holy Spirit for help. This is when I had to embrace the struggles Katie and I experienced so our marriage could improve. I had to ask my wife the tough questions, such as: "What do we need to do to make this work? What do I need to change? How am I failing you?" I also had to ask her to forgive me for not making her the supreme relationship—second to Christ—the Lord wanted her to be in my life.

Part II: Genesis 1–3

Creation of Marriage and the Fall

Chapter Three

God's Establishment of Adam's Headship

Twice the apostle Paul stated the headship of a husband:

- 1 Corinthians 11:3—But I want you to know that the head of every man is Christ, the head of woman is man, and the head of Christ is God.
- Ephesians 5:23—For the husband is head of the wife, as also Christ is head of the church; and He is the Savior of the body.

Although these verses are found in the New Testament, a husband's headship did not have its beginning under the New Covenant. Neither does male headship have its beginning in the Old Testament under the Old Covenant. It does not even have its beginning at the fall.

Male headship actually had its beginning at creation itself. This is important, because if we think headship began after the fall, then this leadership becomes part of sin's curse. If we understand that man's headship began at creation, we will see it as part of God's natural, healthy, divine plan for husbands and wives.

Genesis 1:1 says, "In the beginning God created the heavens and the earth," and the rest of the chapter gives an overview of all six days of creation. God created man and woman on the sixth day. Then, in Genesis 2:7–25, God zooms in on the creation of Adam and Eve since mankind is the pinnacle of God's creation. We are so familiar with the account that it is easy to miss the significance of some of the details. Therefore, let's approach this passage as though we are reading it for the first time. It is in this account that God established man's headship.

Since God created the animals in pairs, male and female, what would we expect Him to do with the creation of humankind? We would expect Him to create the first man and woman at the same time—as a pair, male and female. But that is not what He did, and in creating man first and woman second, God revealed a number of important details.

God's First Command

After God created Adam, He placed him in the Garden of Eden to work (Genesis 2:15). Creating Adam before Eve allowed God to give His first command to Adam alone. Genesis 2:16–17 says:

> And the LORD God commanded the man, saying, "Of every tree of the garden you may freely eat; but of the tree of the knowledge of good and evil you shall not eat, for in the day that you eat of it you shall surely die."

God gave the command to Adam as he stood there alone. Managing the garden was his duty, but when Eve was eventually fashioned, he had the responsibility of passing along to her what he had learned from God. Then Eve had the responsibility of trusting her husband's account. God did not have to do it this way. He could have given the command to both of them after Eve was created, but in doing it this way, God established Adam's headship in the relationship.

Adam Names the Animals and Eve

God had Adam name the animals, which disclosed his lack of a companion. Genesis 2:19–20 says:

> Out of the ground the LORD God formed every beast of the field and every bird of the air, and brought them to Adam to see what he would call them. And whatever Adam called each living creature, that was its name. So Adam gave names to all cattle, to

the birds of the air, and to every beast of the field. But for Adam there was not found a helper comparable to him.

Again, we see God do something with Adam that He could have had Adam and Eve do together. There are two reasons for this. In Genesis 1:26, God said:

Let Us make man in Our image, according to Our likeness; let them have dominion over the fish of the sea, over the birds of the air, and over the cattle, over all the earth and over every creeping thing that creeps on the earth.

First, God wanted man to have authority over creation, and He established that authority by directing Adam to name the animals. Second, instead of simply giving Adam a helper or telling him he should desire one, God chose to reveal this lack to him by bringing the animals to him in pairs. Adam quickly noticed that the animals were in pairs, but he himself was not part of any pair! As Genesis 2:20 describes, he noticed there was no "helper comparable to him."

With Adam now longing for a mate, God was ready to fashion Eve. Here again, familiarity may cause us to miss the significance of certain details. Up to this point, one recurring theme has been God's creation of living things from ordinary dirt:

- Genesis 2:7—And the LORD God formed man *of the dust of the ground*, and breathed into his nostrils the breath of life; and man became a living being.
- Genesis 2:9—And *out of the ground* the LORD God made every tree grow.
- Genesis 2:19—*Out of the ground* the LORD God formed every beast of the field and every bird of the air.

With this repetition, we would expect to read: "The LORD God formed woman *of the dust of the ground*, and breathed into her nostrils the breath of life; and woman became a living being." Instead, Genesis 2:21–23 says:

And the LORD God caused a deep sleep to fall on Adam, and he slept; and He took one of his ribs, and closed up the flesh in its place. Then the rib which the LORD God had taken from man He made into a woman, and He brought her to the man. And Adam said: "This is now bone of my bones and flesh of my flesh; she shall be called Woman, because she was taken out of Man."

Earlier, God brought the animals to Adam to be named, demonstrating Adam's authority over them. Adam then named his wife, demonstrating his authority over her: "She shall be called Woman." This is one more indication of God establishing Adam's headship within the marriage relationship.

History's First Surgery

God performed history's first surgery by using Adam's body to fashion Eve, and what modern science reveals about this is fascinating. Every cell in our bodies contains our entire genetic blueprint or DNA. Therefore, God could take some of Adam's cells and use their DNA to create Eve. The reverse, however, would not have been possible, because men's DNA contains both X and Y chromosomes (XY), while women's DNA contains only X chromosomes (XX). If God had created woman first, it would have been impossible to create man, because there would be no Y chromosomes, which is the chromosome that determines male gender. Adam had the genetic material—both X and Y chromosomes—for a woman to be created from his DNA, allowing for the reproduction of men and women.

In being fashioned from Adam, Eve has the unique distinction of being the only part of creation not created out of the ground. Since Adam was created in the image and likeness of God, Eve was just as wonderfully created in the image and likeness of God. It should also be pointed out that while God created woman from man, He brought forth every other human being since Eve from woman. The apostle Paul explained it like this:

For man is not from woman, but woman from man. Nor was man created for the woman, but woman for the man . . . Nevertheless, neither is man independent of woman, nor woman independent of man, in the Lord. For as woman came from man, even so man also comes through woman (1 Corinthians 11:8–9, 11–12).

A final detail of significance is that God's creation of woman from man involved far more than Adam's rib. The Hebrew word for rib is *tsela*. The word occurs forty-one times in the Old Testament, but only here in Genesis 2:21–22 is it translated "rib." Nineteen times *tsela* is translated as "side" and eleven times as "chamber." Here are a few examples:

- Exodus 25:12—You shall cast four rings of gold for [the ark], and put them in its four corners; two rings shall be on one side (*tsela*), and two rings on the other side (*tsela*).
- 2 Samuel 16:13—And as David and his men went along the road, Shimei went along the hillside (*tsela*) opposite him and cursed as he went.
- 1 Kings 6:8—The doorway for the middle story was on the right side (*tsela*) of the temple.

Eve came from Adam's side, not only from his rib, which is also made clear in Adam's words in Genesis 2:23 when he calls Eve "bone of my bones and flesh of my flesh."

Why did God choose to create Eve from Adam's side instead of creating her from the dust of the ground like everything else? God wanted Adam and Eve to understand the unity between them. This is why the next verse, Genesis 2:24, says, "Therefore a man shall leave his father and mother and be joined to his wife, and they shall become one flesh." This is a very odd statement since Adam and Eve are the only two people in history with no "father and mother." Therefore, this verse is not primarily about them but is instructive for all future marriages.

Genesis 2:24 further supports male headship. Why does the command mention a man leaving his father and mother but not a woman leaving her father and mother? It is because the man is moving out from under his parents' authority and establishing his own headship—or authority—over his family. But the woman is not doing the same. She is simply moving from being under her father to being under her husband.

This is why 1 Corinthians 11:3 does not say, "The head of every man and woman is Christ." Instead, it states, "The head of every man is Christ [and] the head of woman is man." Women remain under a man's authority, first her father's and then her husband's, and these men are under Christ. This biblical principle is played out at weddings symbolically when the father walks his daughter down the aisle and gives her to the man who is about to become her husband. The image is of a transfer of authority from father to husband.

Egalitarianism Versus Complementarianism

Egalitarianism is the rejection of the authority God established between husbands and wives. Egalitarians believe God does not have separate and distinct plans for men and women but that they are interchangeable in terms of their roles and responsibilities. Homosexual marriage, transgenderism, and bisexuality are simply extreme forms of egalitarianism.

The Scripture most cited by egalitarians is Galatians 3:28: "There is neither Jew nor Greek, there is neither slave nor free, *there is neither male nor female*; for you are all one in Christ Jesus." Using the verse to support egalitarianism is taking it out of context because it deals with salvation. Everyone, whether Jew, Gentile, slave, free, male, or female is saved in the same manner—by grace through faith apart from the law and works (Galatians 3:1–25). If Paul were saying men and women are identical in terms of responsibilities, he would be contradicting numerous Scriptures he wrote outlining the differences between the gender roles.

Bible scholar James Fowler explains:

Egalitarian assertions are based on false premises. [Identical] responsibilities and authority produces the chaos of no one having ultimate authority or responsibility. The egalitarian premises of socialistic communism are unworkable. Identity, value and worth are not found in gender function, but in a personal Being beyond ourselves.[2]

Complementarianism, on the other hand, teaches that God has separate and distinct responsibilities for men and women that allow them to balance and support each other. Complementarians recognize the gender roles in Scripture are meaningful and, when embraced, promote spiritual and emotional health that allows people to reach their God-given potential.

Scripture says, "God created man in His own image; in the image of God He created him; male and female He created them" (Genesis 1:27, 5:2; Mark 10:6). The emphasis is not on God's creating people but on His creating two different types of humans: one male and one female. The rest of Scripture goes on to reveal the distinct plans God has for each. Although men and women equally share God's image and together have dominion over creation, God designed them differently in order to accomplish His purposes.

A common criticism of complementarianism is that it is chauvinistic in that it identifies one gender as superior to the other. Egalitarians will insist a difference in roles and responsibilities implies a difference in equality, but two people can be different and equal. Men and women can have the same value and significance while not being identical in their roles or responsibilities. God's very nature supports this in that there are three different Persons with distinct roles, but there is still equality.[3]

Pastor David Guzik states:

In our day, many say there is no real difference between men and women. This makes sense if we are the result of mindless evolution, but the Bible says "male and female He created them."

[2] James Fowler. "Women in the Church." Christ In Your Ministries. 1999. Accessed March 7, 2016. http://www.christinyou.net/pages/womeninchurch.html.

[3] Read more about this in Chapter 13.

To God, the differences between men and women are not accidents. Since He created them, the differences are good and meaningful. One of the saddest signs of our culture's depravity is the amount and the degree of gender confusion today. It is vain to wonder if men or women are superior to the other. A man is absolutely superior at being a man. A woman is absolutely superior at being a woman. But when a man tries to be a woman or a woman tries to be a man, you have something inferior.[4]

We should never expect the secular world to agree with God's Word and accept complementarianism. The real tragedy, though, is when Christians hold to an egalitarian view, seeing no differences between men and women's roles in the home or the church. Such individuals may not condone such outright sins as homosexuality and transgenderism, but they will subtly support these agendas as they deny gender roles and undermine God's Word.

Just as men are needed in the home and the church in crucial ways, so women are needed in the home and the church in crucial ways. But the way each gender is needed is different, and we must maintain the distinctions between the roles and responsibilities if we are to obey God's Word.

Better Together

We will look at Genesis 2:18 later, but for now it is worth noting God called Eve "a helper comparable to [Adam]" and the Hebrew word for "comparable" is *neged*. Other translations say "suitable for him" (NASB, NIV) and "fit for him" (ESV). The literal translation actually means "opposite or contrasting."

Men and women were designed to fit perfectly in all ways—physically, emotionally, mentally, and spiritually. When a husband and wife become one flesh on their wedding day, they are two people who complement and

---

[4] David Guzik, "Genesis 1" Enduring Word Media. 2013. Accessed March 7, 2016. http://enduringword.com/commentaries/0101.htm.

complete each other. Together, they become something stronger and more magnificent than they could ever be alone. The strengths of each compensate for the weaknesses of the other:

- When a husband thinks about his wife, he should see her as God's suitable companion for him.
- When a wife thinks about her husband, she should see herself as God's perfect fit for him.

We should give thanks to God for His wonderful design and do everything we can to fulfill the roles He has given us as husband and wife.

Chapter Four

Male Leadership Is God's Pattern

The pattern of male leadership in the community of faith began at creation and is maintained throughout Scripture:

- There were patriarchs instead of matriarchs.
- The tribes of Israel were named after men.
- The only legitimate mediators between God and people were men (i.e., priests instead of priestesses).
- God appointed kings instead of queens.
- God called men to be the focal points of His covenants with mankind (i.e., Adam, Noah, Abraham, Moses, David, and Jesus).

So why do we see examples of female leadership in Scripture? What about queens, prophetesses, at least one female judge—Deborah? Were these women an anomaly? Are they examples of rebellion against God's design, or is there another explanation? To answer these questions, let's look at them individually.

Queens

Scripture mentions three prominent queens, and they fall into two categories. Jezebel (1 Kings 16–22; 2 Kings 9) and Athaliah (2 Kings 8, 11) were evil women who seized control and became tyrannical leaders. Jezebel instituted the worship of the false god Baal across Israel and persecuted followers of Yahweh. Athaliah murdered her grandchildren upon the death of her son and then seized the throne of Judah. Clearly, neither woman serves as a good example.

On the other hand, Esther stands in contrast as a godly queen. She supported male leadership through her submission first to her adopted father, Mordecai, and then to her husband, King Xerxes of Persia. In doing so, God used her to save her entire people from annihilation (Esther 5:1–8, 8:1–8).

Priestesses

Under the Mosaic Covenant, only men could be priests because they were the teachers: "[The priests] may teach the children of Israel all the statutes which the Lord has spoken" (Leviticus 10:11). When female priestesses are mentioned, they are associated with pagan religions such as the worship of Astarte or Baal. Wayne Grudem, professor of theology and co-founder of the Council on Biblical Manhood and Womanhood, explains: "Think of the Bible as a whole, from Genesis to Revelation. Where is there one example in the entire Bible of a woman publicly teaching an assembled group of God's people? There is none."[5]

Prophetesses

No negative association is attached in Scripture to women being prophetesses. They could occupy this office for the simple reason that it was not a position of leadership. Authors John Piper and Wayne Grudem explain:

> It is instructive to note in the Old Testament that some women were prophets, but never priests. It is the priests who had the more settled and established positions of leadership in Israel.

---

[5] Wayne Grudem, *Evangelical Feminism & Biblical Truth* (Crossway, 2012), p. 82.

Prophecy is a different kind of gift from teaching, and when women functioned as prophets they did so with a demeanor and attitude that supported male leadership. Women who had the gift of prophecy did not exercise it in a public forum as male prophets did. The reason for this is that such a public exercise of authority would contradict male headship.[6]

If we consider briefly two examples of the most prominent prophetesses in the Old Testament, we see how they not only do not conflict with male headship but actually support it. The first example is Moses's sister Miriam. After Israel crossed the Red Sea, Moses led the nation in a song of praise (Exodus 15:1–19). Then Miriam did something similar in Exodus 15:20–21, but with an important difference: "Miriam the prophetess, the sister of Aaron, took the timbrel in her hand; and all the women went out after her with timbrels and with dances. And Miriam answered them: 'Sing to the LORD . . . '" Note that Miriam led only the women in singing, as opposed to leading both women and men as her brother had done.

Conversely, consider what happened when Miriam joined Aaron in challenging Moses's leadership. In Numbers 12:2 they claimed, "Has the Lord indeed spoken only through [you]? Has He not spoken through us also?" Apparently, Aaron and Miriam thought they should have some of Moses's authority. God quickly called the people of Israel to the tabernacle of meeting, appeared in the pillar of cloud, rebuked Aaron and Miriam, defended Moses, and gave Miriam leprosy (Numbers 12:4–10).

After Moses interceded for Miriam, her leprosy was removed, but God still commanded that she be put outside the camp for seven days (Numbers 12:13–15). Considering that Aaron engaged in the same sin as Miriam, why was she the only one punished in such a way? While it was bad for Aaron to try to usurp his brother's authority, it was even worse for Miriam, as a woman, to do so.

---

[6] John Piper and Wayne Grudem, *Recovering Biblical Manhood and Womanhood* (Crossway, 2006), p. 217.

Another prominent prophetess was Huldah. During Josiah's restoration of the temple, the Book of the Law (Pentateuch) was discovered. When it was read before Josiah, he was grieved to discover how far his nation had strayed from following God. Tearing his clothes, Josiah sent messengers to "inquire of the Lord" (2 Kings 22:13). Those messengers went to Huldah the prophetess. The significance of Huldah's response is that she did not publicly proclaim God's Word. Rather, she explained it privately to the messengers (2 Kings 22:15–20). She exercised her prophetic ministry in a way that did not obstruct but instead supported male headship.

Numerous other prophetesses are listed throughout Scripture, making clear this was not an anomaly:

- Deborah, who also served as a judge (Judges 4:4)
- The wife of Isaiah the prophet (Isaiah 8:3)
- Anna, who spoke about Jesus's birth in the temple (Luke 2:36–38)
- The four daughters of Philip the evangelist (Acts 21:9)

In each case, however, like Huldah, there is no record of these women having the public ministries of their male counterparts.

Other women are not called prophetesses but are recorded as prophesying:

- Hannah, mother of Samuel the prophet (1 Samuel 2:1–10)
- Elizabeth, mother of John the Baptist (Luke 1:39–45)
- Mary, the mother of Jesus (Luke 1:46–55)

But in each instance, the women prophesied under the headship of a husband or father or, in the case of the widow Anna, the temple's own male leadership.

Deborah the Reluctant Judge

Judges were Israel's primary rulers for almost three-and-a-half centuries. They also commanded armies, making them some of the strongest leaders in Scripture. So why did Deborah serve as judge? Her position is often the first brought up to support female leadership. Since Deborah raises understandable confusion, I would like to examine her situation in a little more depth to demonstrate how she also supports the principle of male headship.

Throughout the book of Judges, as men rise to leadership, we read verses identifying them as chosen or empowered by God:

- Judges 3:9—The LORD raised up a deliverer . . . Othniel.
- Judges 3:15—The LORD raised up a deliverer . . . Ehud.
- Judges 6:14—The LORD [said to Gideon], "Go in this might of yours, and you shall save Israel . . . Have I not sent you?"
- Judges 11:29—The Spirit of the LORD came upon Jephthah.
- Judges 13:24–25—Samson . . . grew and the LORD blessed him. And the Spirit of the LORD began to move upon him.

But with Deborah there is no recognition of God's appointing. Judges 4:4 simply says, "Now Deborah, a prophetess, the wife of Lapidoth, was judging Israel at that time." Her introduction emphasizes that she is female, but in a negative light. Wayne Grudem writes:

> Judges 4:4 suggests some amazement at the unusual nature of the situation in which a woman actually has to judge Israel, because it piles up a string of redundant words to emphasize that Deborah is a woman. Translating the Hebrew text literally, the verse says, 'And Deborah, a woman, a prophetess, the wife of Lapidoth, she was judging Israel at the time.' Something is abnormal, something is wrong—there are no men to function as judge! This impression is confirmed when we read of Barak's timidity and the rebuke he receives as well as the loss of glory he could have received.[7]

Judges 4:5 says Deborah "would sit under the palm tree . . . And the children of Israel came up to her for judgment." The nation approached her privately. She did not publicly teach the Word of God. Like Huldah and other prophetesses, she is another example of a woman limited to

---

[7] Wayne Grudem, *Evangelical Feminism & Biblical Truth* (Crossway, 2012), p. 134.

private and individual instruction. Even when Deborah calls for Barak, Judges 4:6–7 shows her speaking to him privately:

> Then she sent and called for Barak the son of Abinoam from Kedesh in Naphtali, and said to him, "Has not the LORD God of Israel commanded, 'Go and deploy troops at Mount Tabor; take with you ten thousand men of the sons of Naphtali and of the sons of Zebulun; and against you I will deploy Sisera, the commander of Jabin's army, with his chariots and his multitude at the River Kishon; and I will deliver him into your hand'?"

Let's take note of several phrases in these verses:

- The statement "Has not the LORD God of Israel commanded?" should not be understood as Deborah giving orders to Barak. As a prophetess, Deborah received a word from God and passed it along to Barak, confirming what he already should have known—that God commanded him to lead the army.
- The directive, "Go and deploy troops," is particularly significant because Deborah was judge at the time. She was in the position typically occupied by Israel's commander, but rather than summon or command troops herself, she let Barak know that God had called him to lead.
- The phrase, "against you I will deploy Sisera," clarifies God's plan for Sisera to attack Barak, not Deborah.
- "I will deliver him into your hand" indicates God wanted Barak, and not Deborah, to claim victory over Sisera.

All this shows that even while serving as judge, Deborah affirmed the rightness of male leadership, not only looking to Barak to lead but letting him know this was what God wanted. Sadly, Barak did not step up but instead told Deborah, "If you will go with me, then I will go; but if you will not go with me, I will not go" (Judges 4:8). We recognize something is not right about a man telling a woman, "I will not go to battle unless you go with me."

Not surprisingly, Deborah rebuked Barak's reluctance: "I will surely go with you; nevertheless there will be no glory for you in the journey you are taking, for the LORD will sell Sisera into the hand of a woman" (Judges 4:9). Deborah's prophecy came true. God routed Sisera's army before Barak, but it was a woman, Jael, who ended up defeating the enemy commander (Judges 4:17–22). Barak should not have insisted Deborah accompany him but instead taken leadership himself.

This entire account is not advocating for female leadership but is instead presented as a criticism of Barak. The book of Judges records some of Israel's worst days, and the absence of male leadership is a strong reflection of the time. Deborah's judgeship actually served as a rebuke to the nation regarding the absence of male leadership. Later, during another dark period in Israel's history, the prophet Isaiah asserted that women ruling was a sign of God's judgment: "As for My people, children are their oppressors, *and women rule over them*. O My people! Those who lead you cause you to err, and destroy the way of your paths" (Isaiah 3:12).

Neither the book of Judges nor the account of Deborah and Barak is presented as an example to follow. The book of Judges is largely an example *not* to follow, as it recounts the breakdown of leadership among God's people: "In those days there was no king in Israel; everyone did what was right in his own eyes" (Judges 17:6, 21:25).

Is there application for marriages in this? Definitely:

- When men need their wives to tell them to take the family to church, pray, or read the Word, they are acting like Barak.
- When a wife is urging her husband to lead and a husband resists or prefers that his wife take charge instead, he is following Barak's example.

If there is an example to be followed here, it is Deborah. She encouraged Barak to lead, told him what God desired of him, and rebuked him when he would not take charge. It is also worth noticing what she did not do. When Barak refused to lead, she did not take control of the situation herself but rather let God direct Barak's steps and victory. Her story should motivate women to do what she did, and Barak's failure should motivate men to avoid the mistakes he made.

The Pattern Continues Today

The pattern of male leadership established at creation is maintained throughout the Old Testament and then carried into the New Testament. The Twelve Apostles were men. Jesus could have chosen six men and six women, but He chose all men for these important leadership positions. The Seventy who were sent out after the Twelve were all men (Luke 10:1). Again, though He could have chosen thirty-five men and thirty-five women, Jesus chose all men.

Church elders are identified as men. Consider the qualifications for elders in 1 Timothy 3:1–5: "If a *man* desires the position of a bishop, *he* desires a good work . . . the *husband* of one wife . . . one who rules *his* own house well, having *his* children in submission." We see the same when Paul discusses elders in Titus 1:6, 9: "If a *man* is blameless, the *husband* of one wife . . . holding fast the faithful word as *he* has been taught." When churches have female pastors or elders, they have rejected the teaching of God's Word. God does not recognize women in those positions, because only men can occupy the office.

In 1 Timothy 2:12–14, the apostle Paul instructs: "I do not permit a woman to teach or to have authority over a man, but to be in silence. For Adam was formed first, then Eve. And Adam was not deceived, but the woman being deceived, fell into transgression." The foundation of these verses comes from two truths we already discussed:

1. Adam was created first.
2. Eve was deceived. While it sounds as though Adam is commended for not being deceived and Eve is condemned for being deceived, it is actually the opposite. Eve was not as much at fault because she was deceived while Adam was more at fault because he sinned knowingly.

Sometimes people ask: "Why can't women be in leadership over men in the church or in the home?" It has nothing to do with talent or gifting. Some women are fantastic teachers and leaders, and they should use their skills over other women and children.

What it does have to do with is Adam's being created first and Eve's being deceived. Beyond that, I cannot say because those are the only two reasons Paul gives in 1 Timothy 2:13–14. The real question is not "Why can't women?" The real question—and it is the same question we often face—is: "Will we submit to God's Word?"

Chapter Five

The Help a Man Needs

Genesis 2:18—And the LORD *God said,*
"It is not good that man should be alone.
I will make him a helper comparable to him."

For six straight days, God created dry land, sun, moon, stars, sea creatures, birds, and animals. At the end of each day, "God saw that it was good" (Genesis 1:4, 10, 12, 18, 21, 25). But for the first time in the creation account, in Genesis 2:18, God saw something that was not good—man's being alone.

God's statement is even more interesting when we consider that Adam and Eve had not yet disobeyed. We do not typically think of anything being "not good" until after the fall. Since Adam had not sinned yet, it was not Adam himself who was not good. Neither was it anything he had or had not done that was not good. It was simply Adam's being alone that was not good. Let's understand why it was not—and still is not—good for man to be alone.

1. If man is alone, he does not have the help he needs. Leading and providing for a family is a lot of work. There is a huge load on men's shoulders, and a wife can help lighten that load. This is why the apostle Paul states, "Man was not created for woman, but woman for the man" (1 Corinthians 11:9). A lot of discouragement

can come a man's way, and if he does not receive encouragement from his wife, where will he get it? Yes, there are other resources such as Scripture and relying on the Lord, but if that was all God wanted men to have, He would not have said, "I will make him a helper."

2. Children are one of God's greatest blessings. If man is alone, he cannot fulfill the second command God gave: "Be fruitful and multiply; fill the earth and subdue it" (Genesis 1:28).

3. God has given men and women healthy desires that He wants satisfied within marriage (Hebrews 13:4).[8] Some of these desires go beyond physical intimacy. God creates people as relational beings with emotional, mental, and social longings that are best satisfied in marriage. People can have great friends, but they should not take the place of a spouse. God wants people to have a companion through life, and part of the reason He created marriage is to see that fulfilled.

4. If man is alone, he does not have the benefit of a woman's influence. While it is not always the case, it is common for married men to become gentler and more sensitive. After Katie and I were married, my parents frequently told me how much she influenced me for the better.

5. If man is alone, he will not experience the sanctification of marriage itself. God accomplishes much of the work He wants to do in our lives through marriage. After Scripture and the Holy Spirit, marriage is the greatest way God teaches us forgiveness, sacrifice, patience, dying to self, and the list goes on. When people remain single they can often develop a greater selfishness as they are able to live only for themselves. Once married they should be living for their spouses, and this is wonderfully sanctifying.

---

[8] Read more about this in Chapters 19 and 20.

A nice companion verse to Genesis 2:18 is Proverbs 18:22: "He who finds a wife finds a good thing and obtains favor from the LORD." When a man receives a wife, he should see her this way; he should understand he is not receiving something neutral or amoral. To illustrate how much of a good thing a wife is, consider God's observation when He finished creating the heavens and the earth: "Then God saw everything that He had made, and indeed it was very good. So the evening and the morning were the sixth day" (Genesis 1:31).

This is the end of the sixth day, but earlier in the day, in Genesis 2:18, God observed, "This is not good." What had changed to go from "not good" to "good"? God had created a woman. That is how good women are. That is how much of a good thing a wife is. The addition of a woman can transform something "not good" into "very good."

When a husband thinks about his wife, he should see her as someone who takes him from "not good" to "very good." And when a wife thinks about her husband, she should think about helping him move from "not good" to "very good." She should be treating her husband in such a way that he can see her as "a good thing" and as "favor from the Lord." She should be giving him the help he needs and, most importantly, the help God wants him to have.

A Helper Comparable to Him

The Hebrew word for helper is *ezer*. It means "help" or "one who helps." The word occurs twenty-one times in the Old Testament, including twice in Genesis 2, first in verse 18 and then in verse 20 when Adam named the animals and could not find "a helper comparable to him."

Some women might find it offensive to be identified as their husbands' "helpers," but the title is not a criticism of Eve's insufficiency but an identification of Adam's inadequacy! In the Amplified Bible Genesis 2:18 reads: "Now the LORD God said, 'It is not good [sufficient, satisfactory] that the man should be alone.'" Woman is the helper man needs because he is not sufficient without her! God created woman to remove man's deficiency. Marriage experts and authors Richard and Sharon Phillips explain:

> To call a woman a helper is not to emphasize her weakness, but her strength. Not to label her as superfluous but as essential to Adam's condition and to God's purpose in the world. Helper is a position of dignity given to the woman by God Himself.[9]

Ezer is never used in Scripture for something negative, such as a sycophant, minion, or slave. Instead, it is used to describe great strength and support. Consider these verses:

- Deuteronomy 33:29—Happy are you, O Israel! Who is like you, a people saved by the LORD, the shield of your help (*ezer*) and the sword of your majesty!
- Ezekiel 12:14—I will scatter to every wind all who are around him to help (*ezer*) him, and all his troops.

Considering this context, identifying woman as her husband's *ezer* reveals her as a powerful and influential companion.

God as Our *Ezer*

Eleven of the nineteen times *ezer* is used outside Genesis 2 occur in Psalms. Each time it describes God as our helper. Some examples include:

- Psalm 33:20—Our soul waits for the LORD; He is our help (*ezer*) and our shield.
- Psalm 70:5—Make haste to me, O God! You are my help (*ezer*) and my deliverer.
- Psalm 115:9—O Israel, trust in the LORD; He is their help (*ezer*) and their shield.

The very title used to describe a woman's role is a title used to describe God Himself. Since we do not let the identification of God as our helper

---

[9] Richard and Sharon Phillips, *Holding Hands, Holding Hearts* (P&R, 2006), pp. 26–27.

make us think less of God, we should apply that same thinking to wives as their husbands' helpers.

The Holy Spirit as Our Helper

Helper is also a title given to the Holy Spirit by Jesus in the New Testament when He promised not to abandon the disciples after His departure:

- John 14:16—I will pray the Father, and He will give you another *Helper.*
- John 14:26—The *Helper*, the Holy Spirit, whom the Father will send in My name.
- John 16:7—It is to your advantage that I go away; for if I do not go away, the *Helper* will not come to you.

What a privilege for women to carry the same title given to the Holy Spirit! It is clear that the title of *ezer* or helper is not one of inferiority but of honor.

The Commendable Nature of Helping

Thinking biblically, helping and serving are two of the most admirable actions we can engage in as Christians. Jesus modeled such behavior and called His followers to do the same in Matthew 20:26–28:

Whoever desires to become great among you, let him be your servant. And whoever desires to be first among you, let him be your slave—just as the Son of Man did not come to be served, but to serve, and to give His life a ransom for many.

Few actions are commanded as often in Scripture or look more like Christ than helping and serving. As a result, wives should find it encouraging to be called their husbands' helpers. They should not let society's stereotypes influence their thinking about being a wife. Instead, they should joyfully embrace the role God has given them. Well-known author and speaker on marriage Nancy Campbell says:

[Ladies] are you feeling base and discouraged? Don't listen to these lies any longer. Lift up your head and embrace your mandate from God. You are not working for any earthly employer, but for the King of kings and Lord of lords, the Sovereign God of the universe. When He calls you a helper you can hold your head high.[10]

Help Suited to the Husband

You would think if God called wives to be helpers, He would let them know how to help! But interestingly, there is no list in Scripture telling wives what to do. I suspect this is the case because every man is unique. Since each husband has different strengths and weaknesses, it is impossible to absolutely say how a wife should help because men will want—and need—help in different ways.

Some men love to cook and enjoy taking on that responsibility. For men who struggle just making toast, they will find it helpful for their wives to do the cooking. Some men could not balance a checkbook if their lives depended on it, and for those men, it will be helpful if their wives oversee the finances. For other couples, turning the finances over to the wife would leave accounts overdrawn in a month. The important issue here is for wives to learn what their husbands need and then strive to help in those ways.

Let me share an example from my own life. Much of my ministry revolves around teaching, and Sunday's sermon receives particular attention. I go over it twice each week with Katie and, as a result, I have improved as a preacher. A weakness I had when I started pastoring was sharing a lot of technical information but little in the way of application. My wife has helped me in this area by regularly asking, "What does this

---

[10] Campbell, Nancy. "Do You Feel Downgraded?" Above Rubies. February 12, 2015. Accessed March 7, 2016. http://aboverubies.org/index.php/ar-blogs/entry/do-you-feel-downgraded.

have to do with our lives? How is this going to challenge us in the different roles we find ourselves?"

Katie has also helped me become clearer, letting me know when something is confusing. I might respond, "This is what I was trying to say," and she will say, "That's not how it sounded before. What you just said makes sense." Because of all this, I often say from behind the pulpit, "When I was going over the sermon with Katie . . ." The congregation knows how much my wife helps me, and I often hear people say, "You two make a great team." And they are right. My preaching has improved significantly because of the time and effort Katie has committed to going over my sermons with me.

While I know most women reading this may not have husbands who preach, the principle is still the same. Wives need to look for the unique areas in which their strengths can complement their husbands' needs and weaknesses.

Hopefully a wife will be committed to helping her husband even if it is not what she enjoys doing. Our children often say they want to help, but when we tell them what they can do, they sometimes respond, "This is what I want to do instead." As a result, they end up not being much help at all. Unfortunately, I have seen wives with similar attitudes. They say they want to help their husbands but only if it is the way they want to help. Just as with our children, wives with this attitude end up not being much help to their husbands.

Helping Is a Two-Way Street

One of the most common complaints I hear from wives is, "My husband doesn't communicate with me!" Wives are not mind readers, and husbands can be notorious for giving short and sometimes ambiguous answers. Plenty of wives who want to be good helpers cannot because they do not know what their husbands want. Husbands can help their wives tremendously by communicating with them clearly and more frequently. I will say it like this: Husband, help your wife be your helper by communicating to her how she can help you.

Also, just because God graciously gave Adam a wife to complement him and help meet his needs does not mean that a wife should endlessly serve her husband while he does not lift a finger. Scripture identifies wives as the helper, but husbands also help their wives. There may even be times when a husband is called to take over some of his wife's responsibilities.

As I was writing this book, we learned that Katie was expecting our sixth child. She has a condition called *hyperemesis gravidarum*, which means she gets very sick during pregnancy. During this season, Katie can barely get out of bed some mornings, much less care for five other children eight and under. We homeschool, so they need their work supervised. Our youngest child needs to be watched so she does not fall down the stairs, put something in her mouth that she should not, or find herself crushed by her older brothers wrestling.

By God's grace, my job has a very flexible schedule. On those days (or weeks) when Katie's sickness is the worst, I stay home in the morning and work later in the evenings. I also take over a number of Katie's normal responsibilities. Every time I "play mom," it reminds me to be thankful for my wife.

What Does a Wife's Help Look Like Practically?

A well-known passage reveals what it means—and does not mean—biblically for a wife to be her husband's helper. Proverbs 31 contains what is commonly known as the Virtuous Wife passage. One might say that it is a description of the ideal woman.

Verses 11 and 12 say, "The heart of her husband safely trusts her; so he will have no lack of gain. She does him good and not evil all the days of her life." He trusts her in more ways than one. He knows she is hardworking and does not need someone standing over her shoulder ensuring she is making good use of her time or the family's finances. She is not like women who might spend hours on the phone, the Internet, or in front of the television. He also trusts her faithfulness to him, knowing she is the opposite of the adulterous wife in Proverbs 7:10–23 who entices the foolish young man with the temptation: "For my husband is not at home." He has "no lack of gain" because as his helper she works hard to "[do] him good." The rest of the passage elaborates on the ways the Virtuous Wife cares for her family and others.

Interestingly, this passage was written at a time when women were not only legal possessions of men but their sphere of influence traditionally did not extend beyond the home and raising children. So what this passage includes as attributes of the "perfect woman" stands out in even starker contrast to what one might consider a stereotype of the biblical wife. Proverbs 31:13–16 deal specifically with the Virtuous Wife's job description:

> She seeks wool and flax, and willingly works with her hands. She
> is like the merchant ships, she brings her food from afar. She also
> rises while it is yet night, and provides food for her household,
> and a portion for her maidservants. She considers a field and buys
> it; from her profits she plants a vineyard.

Notice she gathers the materials to take care of her family. She is diligent with her hands and travels to secure the best food for her loved ones. Her hardworking nature is shown in the way she gets up before dawn to have food prepared not just for her family but also for the servants. She is industrious and resourceful as she buys a field and then reinvests the profits to make more money for her family. This is important because it shows that women can also engage in work that provides for their families financially. Men are not the only ones who can make money.

The passage then elaborates on the ways she further takes care of her family, the poor, and herself. Proverbs 31:17–21 states:

> She girds herself with strength, and strengthens her arms. She
> perceives that her merchandise is good, and her lamp does not go
> out by night . . . She extends her hand to the poor. Yes, she
> reaches out her hands to the needy. She is not afraid of snow for
> her household, for all her household is clothed with scarlet. She
> makes tapestry for herself; her clothing is fine linen and purple.

Her hardworking nature allowed her to be a strong, healthy woman. Everything she made for her family, such as food and clothing, was of high quality, and she was willing to work late into the night to produce it. Her inventory was large enough to help those in poverty. She anticipated her family's needs and made sure they were met. While providing for others, she did not neglect to provide high-quality possessions for herself.

Verse 24 says, "She makes linen garments and sells them, and supplies sashes for the merchants." Her efforts bless many—from the poor and needy, to her family, to the leaders and merchants of the city. While all of this was taking place, she was still careful to keep her home a priority. Verse 27 says, "She watches over the ways of her household, and does not eat the bread of idleness." This is one of a number of verses in Scripture that portray an excellent wife as a homemaker. Here is a list of others:

- Proverbs 14:1a—The wise woman builds her house.
- 1 Timothy 5:14—I desire that the younger widows marry, bear children, manage the house.
- Titus 2:3–5—Older women . . . admonish the young women . . . to be homemakers.

The Virtuous Wife is definitely a skilled homemaker, but there are also verses about her industriousness as she makes money outside the home. How do we explain these two investments of time and energy that seem at odds with each other?

She was clearly able to perform these activities (buying fields and selling products) without neglecting the care of her family. She probably engaged in many of these activities from her home. She makes and sells linen garments and supplies sashes for the merchants, but most likely she produces them at home where she can continue to oversee her family's affairs.

Thus, whatever activity a wife participates in outside the home should never take priority over her home or family. A wife's husband, children, or even the home itself should never suffer as a result of any activity she engages in.

One additional reality worth mentioning is that life does not always go the way people expect or desire. I have known couples who would like the wife to stay at home, but unforeseen circumstances, such as the husband's being injured or a financial emergency, required that the wife work outside the home. These couples should never be made to feel condemned because in such situations this is the best way for the wife to serve her household.

The godly character of the Virtuous Wife far outweighs her industriousness or business expertise. Verses 25–26 say, "Strength and honor are her clothing; she shall rejoice in time to come. She opens her mouth with wisdom, and on her tongue is the law of kindness." Strength, honor, joy, wisdom, and kindness make this woman the opposite of the woman that the apostle Paul describes in 1 Timothy 5:13 when he warns women against being "idle, wandering about from house to house, and not only idle but also gossips and busybodies, saying things which they ought not." The Proverbs 31 woman is busy with her own house and her own family's affairs—not the houses or affairs of others.

Praise for Such a Helper

How does the Virtuous Wife's family react to her? Verses 28–29 say, "Her children rise up and call her blessed; her husband also, and he praises her: 'Many daughters have done well, but you excel them all.'" There are not many satisfactions a woman can enjoy more than receiving her husband and children's praise for her diligence in caring for them. As a result, they have great appreciation for her.

Verse 30 summarizes: "Charm is deceitful and beauty is passing, but a woman who fears the LORD, she shall be praised." Of all that can be said about the Virtuous Wife, this is the highest compliment, indicating she is as strong and impressive spiritually as she is in all other areas. Holiness and godly character deserve more respect than any amount of charisma or physical beauty.

This passage concludes in verse 31: "Give her of the fruit of her hands, and let her own works praise her in the gates." While the passage is instructive for women, it is a strong admonition to husbands to appreciate their wives for their excellence and effort. She has done so much for others that she in turn should be thanked and rewarded for what she has done.

The reference to "the gates" in our day might be similar to putting a notice in the local newspaper or community bulletin board. Back then, the gates were where the leaders of the city sat in session and where the news and commerce were centered. Earlier in the passage, we were told that the Virtuous Wife's husband "is known in the gates when he sits among the elders of the land" (31:23). He is a well-known leader in the community and, by implication, part of his good reputation is the result of his wife's good reputation.

But a loving husband does not just bask in his wife's good reputation. The implication here is that he openly brags about her to his fellow leaders because of the wonderful helper she has been. We husbands should never complain about our wives, but rather make a point to praise them to others.

Chapter Six

Consequences of the Fall for Husbands and Wives

Mankind's first temptation involved the devil's attack on Adam's headship in his relationship with Eve. Genesis 3:1–4 says:

> Now the serpent was more cunning than any beast of the field which the LORD God had made. And he *said to the woman*, "Has God indeed said, 'You shall not eat of every tree of the garden'?" And the woman said to the serpent, "We may eat the fruit of the trees of the garden; but of the fruit of the tree which is in the midst of the garden, God has said, 'You shall not eat it, nor shall you touch it, lest you die.'"
> Then the serpent *said to the woman*, "You will not surely die."

Note an important contrast here between the creation account in Genesis 2 and the fall in Genesis 3:

- In Genesis 2:16, "the LORD God commanded the man."
- In Genesis 3:1 and 4, "[the serpent] said to the woman."

God spoke to Adam, but the devil spoke to Eve. Why? Because the devil knew Eve was "the weaker vessel" (1 Peter 3:7).[11] Part of the reason God placed Eve under Adam's headship was for her own protection.

---

[11] Chapter 18 explains the meaning of the phrase "weaker vessel."

When the devil tempted Eve, she had two choices:

- She could trust her husband who had given her God's command, thereby submitting to him.
- She could trust the devil, submitting instead to him.

Sadly, Genesis 3:6 reveals her choice: "So when the woman saw that the tree was good for food, that it was pleasant to the eyes, and a tree desirable to make one wise, she took of its fruit and ate. She also gave to her husband with her, and he ate."

At this point, Adam also had two choices:

- He could obey God who gave him the command, thereby submitting to Him.
- He could obey his wife, submitting instead to her.

Adam chose to obey his wife instead of obeying God. Genesis 3:9–12 gives us the outcome of that decision:

> Then the LORD God called to Adam and said to him, "Where are you?"
> So he said, "I heard Your voice in the garden, and I was afraid because I was naked; and I hid myself."
> And He said, "Who told you that you were naked? Have you eaten from the tree of which I commanded you that you should not eat?"
> Then the man said, "The woman whom You gave to be with me, she gave me of the tree, and I ate."

It is significant that this conversation about the fall took place between God and Adam. God did not address Eve until Genesis 3:16 when He explained how sin's curse would affect women. God went to Adam because—as the New Testament reveals—He held him more responsible for the fall:

- Romans 5:12–19—Through one man sin entered the world . . . death reigned from Adam . . . the transgression of Adam . . . by the one man's offense many died . . . by one man's offense death reigned . . . through one man's offense judgment came . . . by one man's disobedience.

- 1 Corinthians 15:21–22—By man came death . . . In Adam all die.

Since Eve sinned first, we would expect to read that sin and death entered the world through her, but God placed the blame squarely on Adam's shoulders. Why? As recipient of God's command and head of the relationship, Adam had higher accountability. So how does all this apply to husbands and wives?

- Wives should consider how poorly it went for Eve when she stepped out from under Adam's headship. While staying under a husband's headship is no guarantee everything will go perfectly, wives can be encouraged that this is God's plan for their own best interests and safety. By staying under their husbands' headship, wives are placing themselves in positions for God to work through and bless their obedience.

- Husbands note that even though Eve made the initial wrong choice, the sobering fact is that God still held Adam responsible! This should serve as a warning to all husbands regarding the accountability that is on our shoulders. When God confronted Adam, he tried to blame Eve (Genesis 3:12). But it did not work for Adam, and it does not work today for husbands to blame their wives. As God-appointed heads of the relationship, husbands will be held responsible for what takes place in our marriages and in our homes.

The Results of Adam and Eve's Disobedience

Prior to the fall, Adam and Eve lived in perfect harmony with each other, but sin introduced conflict. The fall affected both sides of the marriage relationship. Before banishing Adam and Eve from the Garden of Eden, God revealed what their relationship would now be like living in a fallen world. Genesis 3:16–17 records:

To the woman He said: "I will greatly multiply your sorrow and your conception; In pain you shall bring forth children; *Your desire shall be for your husband, and he shall rule over you.*"
Then to Adam He said, "*Because you have heeded the voice of your wife,* and have eaten from the tree of which I commanded you, saying, 'You shall not eat of it.'"

The italicized words identify the three specific struggles—or temptations—husbands and wives face as a result of our acquired sin natures. Let's look at each of them.

A Wife's Temptation to Control Her Husband

The phrase, "Your desire shall be for your husband" refers to a wife's desire to control her husband. Before the fall, Eve would have willingly and eagerly submitted to Adam, but now she will want to resist his headship and control him instead.

How do we know this is what is meant in the verse? First, this is a curse and not a blessing. It cannot mean wives are going to love their husbands or desire them in some positive way. Second, a basic rule of Bible interpretation involves considering the meaning of words by looking at the way they are used elsewhere in Scripture. Whenever possible, an example from the same book of the Bible is preferred, because often the author and time of writing will be the same for both uses. The Hebrew word for "desire" is *teshuwqah*, and it occurs only three times in Scripture— twice in Genesis and once in Song of Solomon 7:10: "I am my beloved's, and his desire is toward me."

For our purposes, let us consider the second usage of *teshuwqah* in Genesis, just before Adam and Eve's firstborn son, Cain, murdered his brother, Abel:

Abel also brought of the firstborn of his flock and of their fat. And the Lord respected Abel and his offering, but He did not respect Cain and his offering. And Cain was very angry, and his countenance fell.
So the Lord said to Cain, "Why are you angry? And why has your countenance fallen? If you do well, will you not be accepted? And

if you do not do well, sin lies at the door. And *its desire (teshuwqah) is for you*, but you should rule over it."
Now Cain talked with Abel his brother; and it came to pass, when they were in the field, that Cain rose up against Abel his brother and killed him (Genesis 4:4–8).

When God rejected Cain's offering, Cain faced the two choices we all face when rebuked. We can be humble, repent, and do what is right, or we can be prideful, angry, and pout, thereby allowing sin to remain in our lives. As God graciously warns Cain about what sin wants to do to him, the parallelism with Genesis 3:16 is obvious:

- Genesis 3:16—Your desire (*teshuwqah*) shall be for your husband, and he shall rule (*mashal*) over you.
- Genesis 4:7—[Sin's] desire (*teshuwqah*) is for you, but you should rule (*mashal*) over it.

What kind of "desire" did sin have for Cain? Was it a gentle, supportive, affectionate desire? No, it was the desire sin has for everyone—a desire to control Cain's mind and actions. God told Cain he needed to rule over sin, but Cain failed to obey God and instead let sin control him so much that he murdered his brother. The application is this:

- Just as sin had a desire to control Cain, God warned Eve in Genesis 3:16 that wives will have a desire to control their husbands.
- Just as Cain was urged to "rule over" or have authority over sin, so God commands husbands to have authority over their wives.

A Husband's Temptation to Dominate His Wife

The last phrase of Genesis 3:16 introduces the first temptation husbands face: "And he shall rule over you." This may sound as though God is establishing authority in the marriage relationship, but we have already seen that headship was established before the fall. So what is God communicating with these words? He is describing what women will have to endure as a result of the curse. Just as God pointed out the "desire" women would have to control their husbands, so He also pointed out the temptation men would have to control their wives.

As a result of the fall, the Battle of the Sexes is now full-blown. On one side, the conflict has birthed feminism and the women's liberation movement with wives desiring to control their husbands and reject the headship over them. On the other side is male chauvinism with men being harsh, cruel, or domineering. Genesis 3:16 could be understood as a prophecy that wives will have to resist controlling their husbands, and husbands will have to resist being tyrants to their wives.

God called man to lead before the fall. If the fall had never taken place, Eve would have been able to submit to Adam with joy and humility, and Adam would have led with perfect love, compassion, and kindness. After the fall, man is still expected to lead, but now there is conflict where there was previously peace.

A Husband's Temptation to Submit to His Wife

The second temptation husbands face is contained in Genesis 3:17: "Because you have heeded the voice of your wife." When Adam and Eve sinned, they both violated God's divine pattern for marriage by reversing the gender roles:

- Eve usurped her husband's authority by acting independently of him and ignoring the command he had communicated from God.
- Adam abandoned his appointed role as leader in choosing to submit to Eve instead of to God.

As with Adam, the greatest struggle for some husbands is not in being domineering toward their wives but rather being passive. Their greatest temptation is to not lead at all. Both temptations have serious consequences. It is a terrible thing for men to mistreat their wives by being harsh or cruel. But it is also terrible for men to mistreat their wives by not leading.

So which temptation do men surrender to most commonly? That certainly varies widely according to culture. In parts of the world where women still rank as little more than a possession, a more common sin is cruelty toward women. Although there are many abusive men in Western nations where both men and women can claim legal protections, the more common temptation seems to be passivity or laziness.

Why is this the case? A likely assumption is acceptability. In our Western culture, both secular society and the church rightly consider it unacceptable for men to be cruel to women. But it is generally accepted, even within many Christian circles, for men to be passive and lazy when it comes to leading in the home and in the church.

I witnessed a particularly unhappy illustration of this temptation some years back when a married man began attending our church without his wife. I learned that she attended a different church where she occupied a position of leadership and teaching over men and women. "I would like her to go to church with me," he shared, "but she won't."

He wanted me to speak with her, hoping I might convince her to embrace a biblical view of marriage. We began counseling sessions, but when I shared passages instructing wives to submit to their husbands, she would argue and justify not having to obey. During that time the wife's authoritarian personality put her at odds with the church she was attending, so she began accompanying her husband to our church. When I began preaching the same series on marriage I am presenting in this book, she grew so frustrated that her husband told me, "My wife wants to leave the church."

I encouraged him to lead in his marriage, but they left a few months later. The situation could have been avoided if either of them had chosen to obey Scripture. Instead, a passive man would not lead, and a rebellious woman would not submit.

Sadly, their situation parallels the fall in the Garden of Eden when Adam abdicated his leadership role and Eve usurped his authority. It also illustrates what can happen in marriages when husbands and wives fail in their roles. Consequences such as frustration and regret will be an inevitable result.

Ultimately, it is impossible for someone *not* to lead. The only way for nobody to lead is to do absolutely nothing and make absolutely no decisions. But if a couple does anything, however small or insignificant, someone had to take initiative. Someone had to get things moving in a certain direction. If men prefer to be passive and lazy, someone will step into the leadership role. Usually, that ends up being the wife.

Since male headship receives so much criticism from society, and sometimes even from within the church, you would expect the most common complaint from women to be something like: "My husband wants to lead and I hate it. It is so barbaric and chauvinistic. He acts like such a dictator." Actually, the frustration I hear more often as a pastor is just the opposite: "My husband won't lead. I wish he wasn't so passive and lazy!"

God has created women with a desire for a strong leader. Because of the fall women have flesh that bucks against male headship, but they also have a spirit that craves a spiritual man they can follow.

The Consequences for Abraham and Ahab

One of the purposes of the Old Testament is providing examples for us to learn from. Consider these verses:

- Romans 15:4—For whatever things were written before [referring to the Old Testament] were written for our learning, that we through the patience and comfort of the Scriptures might have hope.
- 1 Corinthians 10:11—Now all these things happened to them as examples, and they were written for our admonition, upon whom the ends of the ages have come.

The Old Testament provides a backdrop for New Testament instruction, including on the topic of marriage. So throughout this book we will look at certain individuals in the Old Testament who will help us make practical application of New Testament commands. Sometimes the individuals will serve as positive examples through their obedience, while other times they will serve as negative examples through their disobedience.

Along with Adam, Scripture provides two other instructive examples of men who gave in to the temptation to submit to their wives.

God promised Abraham he would be the father of a nation (Genesis 12:2). Abraham and Sarah could hardly have expected decades to pass before God fulfilled His promise. Because of the long wait, Sarah succumbed to unbelief and a desire to control her husband as we see in Genesis 16:1–2:

> Now Sarai, Abram's wife, had borne him no children. And she had an Egyptian maidservant whose name was Hagar. So Sarai said to Abram, "See now, the LORD has restrained me from bearing children. Please, go in to my maid; perhaps I shall obtain children by her." And *Abram heeded the voice of Sarai.*

Do these words sound familiar?

- Genesis 3:17a—Then to Adam He said, "Because you heeded (*shama*) the voice (*qowl*) of your wife."
- Genesis 16:2b—And Abram heeded (*shama*) the voice (*qowl*) of Sarai.

Abraham faced the same two choices Adam faced: obey God or obey his wife. Sarah usurped Abraham's authority. Abraham submitted to Sarah instead of leading as God commanded. The consequence was conflict between Hagar's son Ishmael and Abraham's God-designated heir, Isaac—a conflict that continued between their descendants and plagues our planet to this very day.

The second example involved Ahab, king of Israel, and his wife, Jezebel, a wicked and tyrannical queen who imposed Baal worship on the Israelite people. Ahab was just as wicked, but he was also spineless. He wanted a vineyard that belonged to a godly man named Naboth. Even though Ahab offered Naboth a substantial amount of money and a better vineyard, Naboth declined (1 Kings 21:3).

This sent Ahab home pouting. When he told Jezebel what was wrong, she had an immediate solution: "You now exercise authority over Israel! Arise, eat food, and let your heart be cheerful; I will give you the vineyard of Naboth the Jezreelite" (1 Kings 21:7). Tragically, Jezebel had Naboth murdered. When Jezebel informed Ahab of her success, he jumped into his chariot and headed gleefully off to take possession of his new property (1 Kings 21:8–15).

Since Jezebel had Naboth murdered, would God hold Ahab responsible? We find the answer when the prophet Elijah caught up to Ahab at Naboth's vineyard: "Thus says the LORD: '*Have you murdered* and also taken possession? In the place where dogs licked the blood of Naboth, dogs shall lick your blood, even yours'" (1 Kings 21:19). God held Ahab responsible for Naboth's murder, just as God held Adam responsible for eating from the Tree.

Ahab and Jezebel's marriage is summarized in 1 Kings 21:25: "There was no one like Ahab who sold himself to do wickedness in the sight of the LORD, *because Jezebel his wife stirred him up.*" This summary should be sobering to husbands and wives:

- Jezebel shows wives the great influence they can be in their husbands' lives. Women can follow her example, or they can stir up their husbands to do good.
- Husbands should notice that though Jezebel influenced Ahab to wickedness, God still held Ahab responsible for yielding to his wife. Whether it is Adam, Abraham, or Ahab, God appointed men to lead, and they cannot turn around and say, "My wife made me do it." God is going to hold men responsible for what happens in their marriages.

Reversing the Effects of the Fall

Husbands and wives were designed to be lifelong companions, but now sinful natures are at work, trying to destroy what God has joined together.

Sin has turned God's ordained roles into struggles of pride, selfishness, and self-will. How can a marriage survive this kind of conflict?

The good news is that we have been given a recipe for reversing the effects of the fall, and it is in the commands God has given us in His Word:

- God's commands can take harsh or passive men and make them loving, godly leaders.
- God's commands can take controlling, manipulative women, and make them gentle and respectful.

The result will be relationships characterized by love, joy, and peace. In the chapters that follow, we will look at these commands and how we can apply them to enjoy a marriage such as God intended for Adam and Eve before the fall.

Part III:

Understanding Love

Chapter Seven

What Is Love?

*Ephesians 5:25—Husbands, love your wives, just as Christ
also loved the church and gave Himself for her.*

*Titus 2:4—Admonish the young women to
love their husbands.*

The English language has a single word for "love." A man uses the
same word to say he loves football, working on his car, and his wife.
For his wife's sake, let's hope he loves her differently from the way he
loves football or automobiles. A wife in turn might say that she loves
shopping, her husband, and her children. Obviously, the love we have for
things we enjoy is different from the love we experience in relationships.
And even within our relationships, we recognize we love our parents
differently from the way we love our spouses. We love our children
differently from the way we love our pastors or fellow church members,
our co-workers, or our clients.

Within marriage, the question is what kind of love should a husband
have for his wife? Or a wife for her husband? What does that love look
like? If spouses are to obey God's command to love each other, they
obviously have to be able to answer these questions. The New Testament
is written almost entirely in Greek, a language that contains four different
words for love: *eros, phileo, storge,* and *agape.* Let's define and examine a
biblical picture of each. With an understanding of three of the words for

love—*eros*, *storge*, and *phileo*—we will be better prepared to understand the superior form of love: *agape*.

Why is it so important to understand *agape*? It occurs twice in Ephesians 5:25 when Paul says, "Husbands, love (*agape*) your wives, just as Christ also loved (*agape*) the church and gave Himself for her." *Agape* is the love husbands are commanded to have for their wives, and it is the love Christ has for His bride, the church. It is also the love God has for each of us: "For God so loved (*agape*) the world . . ." (John 3:16). Therefore, we have to understand *agape* so husbands know how to love their wives, so wives know how they should be loved by their husbands, and so we can all understand the love God the Father and God the Son have for us.

Eros—Physical Attraction

Eros is the only Greek term for love that is not referenced directly in Scripture. The word refers specifically to physical attraction or romantic love. We will discuss it more fully in Chapter 19 when covering physical intimacy.

Storge—Natural Affection

Storge refers to natural affection, or familial love, such as the way a parent feels toward a child or the way siblings feel toward each other. The word *storge* is not used in Scripture in its simple form, but the word *astorgos* is used twice. *Astorgos* is *storge* with an "a" in front of it, making it the opposite—without love or without natural affection. The apostle Paul uses it when he states that people will not "retain God in their knowledge [therefore He] gave them over to a debased mind, to do those things which are not fitting; being filled with all unrighteousness [including being] unloving (*astorgos*)" (Romans 1:28, 31). Paul uses the word again when he writes to Timothy: "In the last days perilous times will come: for men will be . . . unloving" (2 Timothy 3:1, 3).

In both instances Paul was not simply saying that people are unloving. He was saying people will lack the natural love or affection family members should have toward each other. A biblical example of *astorgos* (the absence of *storge*) would be Cain's murdering Abel. A present-day example would be mothers' murdering their babies in the womb. An abortion is the height of *astorgos*, or lacking natural love, because even in nature mothers fiercely protect their offspring.

Storge is also used once in Scripture in combination with a third form of love, *phileo*: "Be kindly affectionate to one another with brotherly love" (Romans 12:10). The words "kindly affectionate" are a translation of *philostorgus* in the original Greek, a word that combines *phileo* and *storge*. Within the context of Romans 12, it is referencing the family affection brothers and sisters in Christ should have for each other.

Phileo—Strong Affection

Phileo can be defined as strong affection. Most commonly, this applies to affection or kindness between friends. When Jesus wept at Lazarus's death in John 11:36 the Jews said, "See how He loved (*phileo*) him!" *Phileo* also forms part of the words "philosophy," an affection for wisdom, or "philanthropy," an affection for fellow man. The church of Philadelphia, mentioned in Revelation 3:7–13, literally means "the church of brotherly love." When people consider themselves close friends, *phileo* is the affection they have for each other.

It is natural to focus on the romance—or *eros*—of marriage. But in doing so, we forget that marriage should actually be the union of two best friends. In many ways, *phileo* is a great description of what marriage should be: a deep and close friendship. Your spouse should be your best friend. I am always sad when I see people who are closer friends with others than with their spouses. It is tragic when people say, "Oh, my spouse is leaving for a week. I can't wait. What a wonderful break!" If a husband or wife ever feels this way toward the other, they should pray that God restores or increases the *phileo* in their relationship.

But *phileo* does not always have a positive connotation. In Matthew 6:5, Jesus accuses: "[The religious leaders] love (*phileo*) to pray standing in the synagogues and on the corners of the streets." Their strong affection was directed at receiving the adoration of men.

Agape—A Superior Love

The fourth form of love—and the most commonly mentioned in the New Testament—is *agape*. A conversation between Jesus and Peter reveals its superior nature.

The background to this discussion was Peter's earlier pledge to lay down his life for Jesus (John 13:36–38). Even when Jesus warned Peter that he would deny Jesus three times, Peter vowed his unswerving love. In fact, he boasted, "Even if all the other disciples deny You, I will not!" But sure enough, when Jesus was arrested, Peter ran to save his own skin and denied three times ever knowing Jesus. During Peter's third denial, Scripture tells us Peter made eye contact with Jesus (Luke 22:59–62). We are not told what Peter saw in that brief look from Jesus, but it was enough to send Peter stumbling out, weeping bitterly. I doubt there was a lower point in Peter's life.

By John 21, Peter has learned of Jesus's resurrection and at least twice had been with the other disciples when Jesus appeared to them (John 20:19–31). But the shame and anguish of his betrayal must have remained a heavy burden. So it is significant in John 21 that when the disciples went out fishing and recognized that the man calling to them from the beach was Jesus, Peter immediately dived into the water and swam to shore. What happened between Jesus and Peter was not recorded, but by the time the rest of the disciples joined them on the beach to eat, there had clearly been reconciliation and forgiveness.

John 21:15a—So when they had eaten breakfast, Jesus said to Simon Peter, "Simon, son of Jonah, do you love (*agape*) Me more than these?"

In asking if Peter loves Him more than *these*, Jesus could be referencing the fish, which would be akin to, "Do you love me more than fishing?" Or He might be referencing the other disciples, in which case Jesus would be asking, "Do you love me more than you love these other disciples?" But based on Peter's earlier prideful declaration, I think Jesus was asking, "Do you love me more than these other disciples love me?" Peter had declared he loved Jesus more than anyone else, and now Jesus was asking if Peter still believed that to be true. Regardless of intent, Jesus was questioning Peter's love for Him, and the word He used was *agape*. Now look at Peter's response.

> John 21:15b—[Peter] said to Him, "Yes, Lord; You know that I love (*phileo*) You."
> [Jesus] said to him, "Feed My lambs."

At this point, Peter was well aware of how he has failed his Master and was so humbled by this realization that he responded with the word *phileo* instead of *agape*. He knew that his previous actions prevented him from being able to claim the superior form of love Jesus was asking about.

> John 21:16—[Jesus] said to [Peter] again a second time, "Simon, son of Jonah, do you love (*agape*) Me?"
> [Peter] said to [Jesus], "Yes, Lord; You know that I love (*phileo*) You."
> [Jesus] said to [Peter], "Tend My sheep."

As though to make His question easier, this time Jesus dropped the phrase "more than these." But He still used the word *agape*, and again Peter responded with the word *phileo*.

> John 21:17a—[Jesus] said to him the third time, "Simon, son of Jonah, do you love (*phileo*) Me?" Peter was grieved because He said to him the third time, "Do you love (*phileo*) Me?"

This time Jesus also used the word *phileo*. He had stopped asking if Peter had *agape* for Him. The passage tells us that this grieved Peter. In fact, the whole conversation would have been painful to Peter for various reasons. First, Jesus asked Peter three times, "Do you love me?" Those three questions would remind Peter of his three denials. Being asked the same question three times would make Peter think Jesus did not believe his professions of love. Then in the third question, Jesus shifted to the word *phileo* as though calling into question even this inferior love Peter professed for Him. The possibility that Peter did not even possess *phileo* for Jesus broke the disciple's heart.

Perhaps most painfully, throughout this conversation, Jesus did not use the new name He had given Peter (Matthew 16:18). Peter means "rock," signifying strength and a firm foundation. Jesus reverted to calling Peter by his original name, Simon, which implied that Jesus was not seeing Peter at this point as a "rock." Considering Peter's previous arrogance, he undoubtedly needed this reminder of his own weakness and humanity so as not to place so much trust in himself again.

> John 21:17b—And [Peter] said to [Jesus], "Lord, You know all things; You know that I love (*phileo*) You."
> Jesus said to [Peter], "Feed My sheep."

The point to notice in this account is Peter recognized the higher calling associated with *agape*. As a result of his previous denials, he did not feel comfortable telling the Lord he had this sacrificial love for Him.

Finally, Jesus's words to Peter should make us reevaluate our own love for the Lord. I cannot help but picture Jesus asking, "Scott, do you love Me?" When Jesus looks at my life, what kind of love does He see for Him? Is it simply an affectionate *phileo* or a sacrificial, all-encompassing *agape*? Would Jesus have to ask me three times if I love Him to humble me as He did with Peter?

A Wife's *Phileo*

Phileo is the love wives are instructed to have for their husbands. When Titus 2:3–4 commands older women to admonish younger women to love their husbands, the Greek word used is *philandros*, a combination of the words *phileo* and *aner* (the word for husband). So while husbands are commanded to have *agape* for their wives (which we will discuss in detail later), wives are commanded to have *phileo* for their husbands. Why is that? What is the implication of that difference in marriage? Is it that husbands do not want or need that kind of love? Is it that women are not as capable of *agape* as men?

I do not think that is it at all. It is simply that the needs of husbands and wives are different. Most men—myself included—would say it can be very discouraging and trying at times being a husband, father, provider, spiritual leader, and everything else that falls on men's shoulders. What could be more encouraging for a husband than a wife who is also a best friend, regularly lavishing *phileo* on him? Conversely, what could be more discouraging for a husband than a wife who acts more like a mother reprimanding him?

On the other hand, a wife needs the *agape* of her husband, because she lives under his authority. She needs him to treat her with the tender, sacrificial *agape* Christ showed His bride. We have already spoken of the temptation for husbands to be harsh and domineering. How much more so in the day Paul wrote these words when a woman was literally owned by her husband. A husband could demand his wife serve him and meet his every need, but a wife could not in turn demand kindness, concern for her needs, or even basic necessities. To show his wife such love as Christ pours out on the church was a choice husbands had to make of their own free will. It still is. And since such love was not easy or natural to the average husband, then or now, the apostle Paul clearly tells husbands to demonstrate this love toward their wives.

Perhaps there are other reasons God commands *phileo* of a wife and *agape* of a husband that we will not know this side of heaven. But in summary, a husband needs his wife's *phileo*; he needs her to be his best friend. A wife needs her husband's *agape*; she needs him to care for her as his most cherished treasure, not see her as an object or employee to satisfy his needs. She needs him to love her as Christ loved the church. And what does that look like? We'll spend the next few chapters answering this question!

Chapter Eight

Characteristics of *Agape*

U nlike the other forms of love, *agape* is a choice versus an emotion. Two of its characteristics make this clear.

Agape Is Unconditional

Phileo is conditional. Two friends might have *phileo* for each other because of qualities they share or circumstances that bring them together. But if those qualities or circumstances change, their *phileo* for each other might also change.

In contrast, *agape* is unconditional. It is not affected by a person's actions, looks, or possessions. People might successfully create *phileo* in someone else by being a better friend, but *agape* cannot be earned or merited. Nothing can be done to increase or decrease *agape*. It can only be given. *Agape* does not demand reciprocation and is independent of how it is treated in return. *Agape* loves even when rejected, mistreated, or scorned. That is what makes this form of love so unique and distinguishable.

The Old Testament provides a beautiful picture of *agape's* unconditional nature. In fact, if a husband asked me, "Pastor, how far should I be willing to go for my wife?" I would tell him to read the account of the prophet Hosea (Hosea chapters 1 and 3 specifically). His story begins when God tells him to marry a woman named Gomer as an object lesson of God's relationship with Israel: "The LORD said to Hosea: 'Go, take yourself a wife of harlotry and children of harlotry, for the land has committed great harlotry by departing from the LORD" (Hosea 1:2).

We do not know whether Gomer was a harlot when Hosea married her or became one later, but at some point, Gomer left Hosea, either to resume her career as a harlot or to pursue adulterous relationships. Eventually she found herself destitute and either sold herself or was sold into slavery. We know this was a sexual slavery, akin to human trafficking today, because God commanded Hosea: "Go again, love a woman *who is loved by a lover and is committing adultery*" (Hosea 3:1).

In obedience to God, Hosea purchased Gomer back from slavery, and restored her to her position as his wife. It is significant that God did not only instruct Hosea to return to Gomer. He commanded him to love her: "Go again, love a woman . . ." Going back to Gomer after her unfaithfulness would have required an unimaginable amount of forgiveness and grace, but Hosea also had to love her. This is unconditional love. This is *agape*.

Did Hosea obey? Did Gomer respond? The context would indicate that they did since the account is presented as a parallel to the love story between God and His people. Let's see how the story ends: "Afterward the children of Israel [represented by Hosea] shall return and seek the LORD their God . . . I [God] will heal their backsliding, I will love them freely" (Hosea 3:5, 14:4). The parallel shows a repentant bride and a husband who freely loves and forgives. It is a wonderful picture of what can take place in even the most broken marriages when a husband will *agape* his wife. Let me give you an example of such a situation.

Katie and I have some dear friends I'll call Brian and Jennifer, and they gave me permission to share their Hosea and Gomer story. Much of their testimony revolves around Jennifer's unfaithfulness to Brian early in their marriage before they were Christians. Jennifer was running around on Brian, even living with other men for stretches of time. Days went by when Brian did not know where Jennifer was or how she was doing.

As Brian and Jennifer share their testimony, there is one point when Jennifer always becomes emotional. She shares how she had been with some man for a period of time and came home hoping to have pushed Brian far enough that he would divorce her. Jennifer did not know that while she had been away, Brian became a Christian. While Brian recognized the sin in Jennifer's life, he also recognized the sin in his own life. He knew he needed a Savior just as much as Jennifer. As a result, he was willing to forgive her. When Jennifer walked in, Brian was sitting in a chair reading his Bible. Looking up at her, he said simply, "I am so glad you're home. I was very worried about you."

Brian's unconditional love for Jennifer finally won her back. She became a Christian and is one of the godliest women I have ever met. Over the decades of their marriage they have faithfully served Christ and brought Him much glory. God used Brian's *agape* to redeem Jennifer and make her an instrument for His kingdom.

Agape Is Sacrificial

Agape is not about feelings or emotions. It is a choice. It is an act of the will. This is important to keep in mind, because we tend to think love is a feeling. You get shot by Cupid's arrow and then you are "in love." Unfortunately, feelings can come and go.

In contrast, *agape* is about what we are willing to do. First Corinthians 13 is known as the Love Chapter, and in verses 4–7 we read:

> Love suffers long and is kind; love does not envy; love does not parade itself, is not puffed up; does not behave rudely, does not seek its own, is not provoked, thinks no evil; does not rejoice in iniquity, but rejoices in the truth; bears all things, believes all things, hopes all things, endures all things.

How many words here describe feelings and emotions? None! How many words are verbs or action words describing what love is willing to do? All of them. Jesus told a parable in Luke 10:25–37 that perfectly illustrates the sacrificial nature of agape. The prelude to this story is that a lawyer sought to test Jesus: "Teacher, what shall I do to inherit eternal life?"

"What is written in the law?" Jesus asked.

In response, the lawyer quoted two well-known Old Testament passages: "You shall love (agape) the Lord your God with all your heart, with all your soul, with all your strength, and with all your mind (Deuteronomy 6:5)" and "love (agape) your neighbor as yourself" (Leviticus 19:18).

"You have answered rightly," Jesus assured the lawyer. "Do this and you will live."

The lawyer understood that to receive eternal life, he needed to have agape for God and his neighbors. But agape is something nobody can exercise perfectly, which could be why the lawyer tried to justify himself by asking another question: "And who is my neighbor?"

Jesus never specifically answered the question but instead told The Parable of the Good Samaritan to illustrate what agape looks like. A man traveling from Jerusalem to Jericho was set upon by thieves, robbed of his clothes, and left half-dead. A Jewish priest and Levite in turn passed by but did not bother to help. Then a Samaritan, both a foreigner and historic enemy to the Jews, saw the man. With compassion, he tended the man's wounds, set the man on his donkey, and took him to a nearby inn where he left funds to cover the man's care.

Jesus then asked the lawyer, "So which of these three do you think was neighbor to him who fell among the thieves?" His question could as easily be phrased: "Which of these three do you think showed agape?" Let's consider how this parable depicts agape:

1. The Samaritan's love was not conditional on anything the wounded man had done for him. In the story, the man was clearly a stranger. So why did the Samaritan help him? Was it all the good times they had shared together? All the wonderful things the injured man had done for him in the past? Some expectation the man would pay the Samaritan back in the future? No. The man had done absolutely nothing for the Samaritan, and the Samaritan

did not expect anything in return. That is the unconditional nature of *agape*.

2.   The Samaritan's *agape* is shown in that he loved a man who despised him. Jews hated Samaritans, but the Samaritan was willing to help the man anyway. *Agape* loves even when it is rejected.

3.   The Samaritan's actions reveal the sacrificial nature of *agape*. He bandaged the man's wounds. There were no first aid kits in those days, so he must have made the bandages from his clothes. He used oil and wine to clean the wounds. He put the man on his animal and walked to the inn where he paid the man's bill and promised to pay even more in the future if needed. All this took time, effort, and money. *Agape* is demonstrated not by words but by sacrifice and actions.

Agape Is God's Love for Man

First John 4:8 and 16 tell us, "God is love (*agape*)." He is the embodiment of *agape*. One of Scripture's most famous verses describe God's *agape* for us: "For God so loved (*agape*) the world that He gave His only begotten Son, that whoever believes in Him should not perish but have everlasting life" (John 3:16).

Think of the other ways this verse could be worded: For God so loved the world that He . . . created a beautiful planet for people to enjoy. Or He . . . gave us the wonderful gift of marriage. Or He . . . blesses us with children. Or He . . . established the church so His people could be part of a spiritual family. All these are true statements, but they do not reveal God's *agape* because they lack one of *agape's* required characteristics: sacrifice. The sacrificial nature of God's *agape* is made evident in His willingness to give "His only begotten Son."

Likewise, 1 John 4:10 says, "This is love, not that we loved God, but that He loved us and sent His Son to be the propitiation for our sins." This communicates the unconditional nature of *agape* in that God loved us even when we did not love Him. The words "sent His Son to be the propitiation for our sins," communicate the sacrificial nature of God's *agape*.

Romans 5:8 reveals the same two characteristics of God's *agape* toward us: "God demonstrates His own love toward us in that while we were still sinners, Christ died for us." The unconditional nature of God's *agape* is revealed in the words "while we were still sinners." God loved us when we were in rebellion against Him. Just as God sent Hosea back to Gomer to love her when she was committing physical adultery, so God loved us even when we were living in rebellion against Him and committing spiritual adultery. The words "Christ died for us" reveal the sacrificial nature of God's *agape*.

I never understood well God's unconditional, sacrificial *agape* until I became a father. Children can be cruel. Countless children rebel against their parents, but how do parents respond? I remember a conversation with our oldest child, Rhea, who was seven at the time. She was asking me if I would love her if she did certain things she considered to be terrible. Each time she would start out, "Would you still love me if I . . ."

I finally told her: "Yes, I love you so much, and there is nothing you could ever do that would make me love you any less. Truthfully, I love you so much I don't know how I could even love you more."

When I said this to Rhea, I meant it, and I know other parents would say the same to their children. That is *agape*. The beautiful reality can be revealed when we contrast ourselves with God. If I, a fallen man with imperfect love, can feel this way toward my children, how much greater must God's *agape* be for us, considering His perfection? Considering He is love? I love Rhea because she is my daughter, but the far greater unconditional and sacrificial nature of God's agape was demonstrated when He was willing to sacrifice His Son for unloving sinners who were not then part of the family of God but in active rebellion against Him. That is agape, and that is God's love for us.

Agape Is Man's Love for Sin

Up to this point we have discussed the positive elements of *agape*, but for a full understanding we must know it is used one other way in Scripture. *Agape* also describes the love man has for sin. Interestingly, this usage occurs in the same discussion as God's *agape* in John 3:16. The setting is a late-night meeting between Jesus and a Pharisee, Nicodemus. After explaining God's *agape* for the world in John 3:16, Jesus says just three verses later: "This is the condemnation, that the light has come into the world, and men loved (*agape*) darkness rather than light, because their deeds were evil."

Considering our prior discussion, this usage for *agape* should actually make perfect sense:

- *Agape* loves even when not reciprocated. Man loves sin even though sin does not love in return. In fact, sin does the opposite: "The wages of sin is death" (Romans 6:23). Sin's response to those who love it is death.

- *Agape* loves unconditionally. It is a love that is completely independent of how the object of the love acts toward or treats the one loving it. Thus, man continues to love sin regardless of the guilt, punishment, suffering, or discipline he experiences as a consequence.

- *Agape* loves sacrificially. Think of everything people are willing to give up for sin: health, dignity, jobs, finances, children, parents, marriages, friendships, churches, and even relationships with the Lord. The tragedy is that there is very little man will not sacrifice for sin.

First John 2:15–16 instructs us: "Do not love (*agape*) the world or the things in the world. If anyone loves (*agape*) the world, the love (*agape*) of the Father is not in him. For all that is in the world—the lust of the flesh, the lust of the eyes, and the pride of life—is not of the Father but is of the world." When we give in to these lusts, we choose sin over our spouses. What does this look like? A husband gives in to:

- The lust of the flesh when he gets drunk
- The lust of the eyes when he looks at pornography
- The pride of life when he puts in unnecessary hours at work to receive praise

A wife gives in to:

- The lust of the flesh when she makes purchases behind her husband's back
- The lust of the eyes when she covets the home of a friend
- The pride of life when she embraces the flirtations of a man who is not her husband

When we satisfy these lusts, we demonstrate a greater love for sin than for our spouses. The motivation behind sinning is always selfish, whereas the motivation behind loving one's husband or wife is always the best interests of the spouse. Sinning is an act of the will, but so is love. We choose to love our spouses when we choose not to give in to our flesh.

Part IV: Ephesians 5:25–33

A Husband's Call to Agape and a Wife's Call to Respect

Chapter Nine

A Husband Should *Agape* His Wife

Ephesians 5:25—Husbands, love (agape) your wives, just as
Christ also loved (agape) the church and gave Himself for her.

With a good understanding of *agape*, we are now prepared to move into the primary passage dealing with husbands loving their wives. In Ephesians 5:25, *agape* is used twice to discuss two different relationships:

1. A husband's relationship with his bride
2. Christ's relationship with His own bride, the church

The two words "just as" reveal that the way Christ loves the church and gave Himself for her is the way a husband is commanded to love his wife and give himself for her. A man should model his relationship with his bride after Christ's relationship with His bride. With Christ as the standard for husbands, every man must recognize that he always has more room to grow.

Once again we see revealed in this verse the characteristics of *agape*:

- The words "gave Himself for her" reveal the sacrificial nature of Christ's *agape*. In John 3:16, if God the Father's *agape* for the world is shown in being willing to sacrifice His Son, then in Ephesians 5:25 the Son's *agape* for the church is shown in being willing to be sacrificed. Christ gave everything He had, including His own life.

That is the standard of unreserved, selfless, sacrificial love husbands are commanded to have for their wives.

- The absence of the word "if" demonstrates the unconditional nature of Christ's *agape*. The verse does not say, "Husbands, love your wives IF . . ." Since Christ loves the church unconditionally, a husband is commanded to love his wife unconditionally. Christ loves the church when it does not submit, does not love Him in return, or disrespects Him. A husband should love his wife if she does not submit, does not love him in return, or disrespects him. When a husband is upset with his bride, he needs to remind himself of the love Christ has for His bride, a love that loves regardless of what the bride has or has not done.

Pastor and theologian John MacArthur writes:

What higher motive could there be for the husband to love his wife? By loving her as Christ loved the church, he honors Christ in the most direct and graphic way. He becomes the embodiment of Christ's love to his own wife, a living example to the rest of his family, a channel of blessing to his entire household, and a powerful testimony to a watching world.[12]

So how do we husbands put into daily practice the standard Christ has set? If one hundred people were asked what it looks like for a husband to love his wife, we would likely hear one hundred different answers:

- Buy her expensive jewelry
- Take her to fancy restaurants
- Whisk her away on exotic vacations
- Make sure she lives in an impressive home

In general, the secular world suggests a husband's love for his wife is demonstrated through material accomplishments. This is why a husband can be:

---

[12] John MacArthur, *The Fulfilled Family* (Thomas Nelson, 2005), p. 78.

- A complete failure in the world's eyes while being a great husband in God's eyes
- A great husband in the world's eyes while being a complete failure in God's eyes

The good news—at least for husbands—is that we do not have to buy our wives anything expensive or glamorous to be pleasing to God. The bad news is that spending lots of money is much easier than doing what God requires.

The True Strength Needed

I started lifting weights in college, and for about fifteen years I worked out every day, week after week, month after month. I really only slowed down when I had a family and no longer had the time. Sadly, during that season my physical strength was the only strength I really cared about. The constant goal was adding more pounds to the bar or completing more reps than I did the week before.

Little did I know that only a few years later, physical strength would take a backseat to the mental, emotional, and—most importantly—spiritual strength needed to be a good husband and father. When your family is experiencing a trial and they look to you for strength, the amount you lift in the gym could not be more irrelevant. At that moment, what is needed is mental, emotional, and spiritual strength the family can draw on. A strength that can help lift the family the way it once lifted a barbell.

Likewise, when a wife is discouraged, defeated, or depressed, she does not need a man who can bench press three hundred pounds. She needs a husband who can say: "Please let me pray for you. Would you like me to read a few psalms to you? This is a really difficult time, but with the Lord's help I know we can make it through this."

If a young man asked me if he was ready to get married, I would ask him: "Are you willing to take responsibility when things do not go well in your family? When your family suffers, as the head of your home, are you willing to accept blame? If your answer is 'No,' then you do not yet have the strength necessary to get married." Being a husband requires having the strength to hold up the family when things are difficult and take responsibility when things do not go well.

Certainly, a husband who takes care of his wife physically, emotionally, mentally, and financially may appear to be a very loving husband. These are aspects of loving well, but if he does not take care of his wife spiritually, his love is incomplete. Many husbands will work hard to take care of their wives—and they should. But in my years as a pastor, I have seen more men fail in regards to the spiritual leadership of their homes than in financial provision. In those cases, the couple spends Sunday morning in church, but their marriage the other six days of the week looks little different from the marriages of unbelievers. As the head of the relationship, it is the husband's responsibility to make sure he is establishing a Christian marriage—not just a marriage that calls itself Christian but a marriage that is Christ-centered. This is the spiritual strength that is required.

Agape Includes Sanctifying and Cleansing

The best way to understand this passage is that Ephesians 5:25 commands husbands to love their wives as Christ loved the church. Then the following verses describe what that looks like. Ephesians 5:25 gives the command, and the subsequent verses explain how to obey the command, beginning with Ephesians 5:26: "That he might sanctify and cleanse her with the washing of water by the word."

This verse discusses the effect of Christ's love on His bride. The church is sanctified and cleansed. Since the relationship between Christ and the church is meant to serve as an example for husbands with their wives, this obligates husbands to sanctify and cleanse their wives. A husband is at least partially responsible for the sanctification of his wife. As Christ prepares a pure bride, so husbands must prepare pure wives.

This sanctifying and cleansing takes place through washing by the Word of God:

- In John 15:3, Jesus speaks to the church, setting the example for husbands with their brides: "You are already clean because of the word which I have spoken to you."
- In John 17:17, Jesus prayed: "Sanctify them by Your truth. Your word is truth."

Husbands, let me address you directly. There are a number of ways for you to "wash" your wife with the Word:

- Take your wife consistently to a Bible-teaching church. It is tragic when husbands, who are called to be the spiritual leaders in their marriages, do not make one of the most basic and foundational practices of the Christian life—corporate worship on the Lord's Day—a priority.
- Most churches have Bible studies, whether in Sunday school or home fellowships, that place couples in a position to have God's Word wash over them.
- Husbands can have Christian radio programs playing or simply listen to an audio Bible in the home or while driving.
- Read God's Word with your wife. I have had men tell me, "I don't know how to read the Bible with my wife!" If a man can read, he can read the Bible with his wife. Choose a book and start at chapter 1, verse 1. Whatever verse you stop at is where you pick up next time.
- Make God's Word a priority in your marriage. While I would never say Christians cannot have televisions, it is worth considering what brings a couple together most often. Is it the television, movies, some other activity, or is it the Word of God?

A Husband Sets the Standard for Holiness

A husband living an unholy life cannot help his wife with her holiness. If husbands are commanded to have a sanctifying influence on their wives, it only makes sense that each husband must maintain a high standard of holiness in his own life. It is not the wife's responsibility to establish the spiritual atmosphere of the home. That responsibility belongs to the husband.

Husbands are responsible for:

- What comes into the home and what influences the family
- What the family watches
- What the family listens to
- How the family talks or jokes
- What company the family keeps
- How the family dresses
- How the family spends their time
- What the family does recreationally
- How involved the family is in the church

Without getting too specific, I will say there are definitely some movies, music, clothing, jokes, language, and activities that should not enter our homes. Husbands are the ones who need to make sure such things do not enter the home. If they have entered, husbands have the responsibility to make sure they are removed.

I would like to share something I witness, and let me be clear that this is my own observation rather than a truth from Scripture. I rarely encounter a husband who complains about his wife's lack of holiness, but I have encountered plenty of wives who complain about their husbands' lack of holiness. I hear wives complain about things their husbands watch, listen to, or say, but I do not often hear husbands complain about things their wives watch, listen to, or say.

Similarly, I do not often hear men say: "My wife won't go to church with me . . . join a home fellowship . . . pray or read the Bible with me." But I do hear wives say these things about their husbands. This becomes even more tragic when we consider that husbands are supposed to be setting the standard for holiness in the home. It is terrible when women have to be the spiritual leaders in the relationship hoping their husbands were more spiritual. Terrible, yes, but unfortunately it seems to be common.

A Husband Gets the Wife He Prepares for Himself

Ephesians 5:27 continues the description of Christ sanctifying and cleansing the church: "That He might present her to Himself a glorious church, not having spot or wrinkle or any such thing, but that she should be holy and without blemish." There is a tremendous truth contained in these words. Christ does what He does in verse 26—sanctifying and cleansing the church—so that He can obtain for Himself the glorious church, or bride, described in verse 27 that has no spot or wrinkle but is holy and without blemish. The ESV says, "So that He might present the church to Himself in splendor . . ." Here is the simplest way to sum it all up: *Christ gets the church He prepares for Himself.*

Since this is again a picture for husbands and wives, what else is the apostle Paul implying by this truth? Just as Jesus gets the church He prepares for Himself, husbands generally get the wives they prepare for themselves. Wives respond well to love, holiness, and obedience to God's Word. When husbands treat their wives forgivingly, lovingly, and tenderly, they will generally receive more forgiving, loving, and tender wives. When husbands treat their wives unforgivingly, unlovingly, and harshly, they generally find themselves with wives who are less forgiving, loving, and tender.

Rather than be cruel or harsh toward their wives, some husbands are more likely to be apathetic or indifferent. They take no interest in their wives. They do not invest in their wives. They are often annoyed with them. We will discuss 1 Peter 3 in chapters 15 through 18, but for now it is worth noting that verse 7 commands husbands to "dwell with [their wives] with understanding." Husbands need to make an effort to know or understand their wives. This is what allows wives to blossom and grow. When husbands are uninterested in their wives, they end up with cold, bitter, frustrated wives.

Earlier we talked about a husband's responsibility regarding his wife's sanctification. Another way to look at this is that husbands are responsible for the wives *they get* for themselves! It is a simple equation. If a husband is helping his wife with her sanctification and spiritual cleansing, he is going to get a sanctified and cleansed wife.

So aside from the fact that God commands it, one great reason for a husband to take his wife to church, read the Word with her, pray with her, and help her grow spiritually is that he will receive a more spiritually mature wife. What kind of qualities will be produced as a result? Galatians 5:22–23 record: "the fruit of the Spirit is love, joy, peace, longsuffering, kindness, goodness, faithfulness, gentleness, self-control."

Conversely, husbands who do not lead their wives spiritually will get wives who are less spiritual. What is the opposite of spiritual? Fleshly. Galatians 5:19–22 list the "works of the flesh" and here are just a few: hatred, contentions, jealousies, outbursts of wrath, selfish ambitions, dissensions, envy, even adultery.

How many husbands see these works in their wives because they themselves are poor spiritual leaders? How many wives might be more spiritually mature if their husbands were praying for them, as well as praying and reading the Bible with them? Tragically, I have listened to some husbands talk terribly about their wives when in fact they have simply received the wives they have prepared for themselves.

Galatians 6:7 tells us: "Do not be deceived, God is not mocked; for whatever a man sows, that he will also reap." The context of this verse is giving to the church, but the principle also applies to a husband's relationship with his wife. Husbands generally reap what they sow in marriage. If husbands will invest in their wives by sowing seeds of love and interest, if they will plant spiritual seeds of sanctification, they will reap what they have sown. Let's summarize by keeping two truths in mind:

1. Foremost, husbands ought to sanctify and cleanse their wives because that is what God commands and husbands will be held accountable for doing so.

2. Husbands ought to love their wives and lead them well so that they might have loving, spiritual wives. The good news is that God's command to husbands benefits them as much as it benefits their

wives. A husband who loves his wife as God commands will bring great blessings to himself.

A Husband's Concern for His Wife

Recall Adam's response upon seeing Eve for the first time: "This is now bone of my bones and flesh of my flesh; She shall be called Woman, because she was taken out of Man" (Genesis 2:23). Just as in English, the Hebrew words for man (*iysh*) and woman (*ishshah*) are closely related, revealing Adam recognized his closeness with his wife. Since Adam knew Eve came from him, looking at her was like looking at himself. Loving Eve was like loving himself. When Adam took care of Eve's physical needs, he was caring for his own body—literally, since her body had earlier been his body. Her flesh was his flesh.

There can be little doubt that Paul had Adam and Eve in mind when he wrote the words of Ephesians 5:28–29: "So husbands ought to love their own wives as their own bodies; he who loves his wife loves himself. For no one ever hated his own flesh, but nourishes and cherishes it, just as the Lord does the church." Paul's connection to Adam and Eve becomes even clearer when we consider that he finishes his instruction to husbands by quoting Genesis 2:24 in Ephesians 5:31: "For this reason a man shall leave his father and mother and be joined to his wife, and the two shall become one flesh."

Just as Adam saw Eve as an extension of his own bone and flesh, so God wants husbands to see their wives as extensions of themselves. A husband should care for his wife as well as he cares for himself. Since he views her body as part of his body, when he loves her, he is loving himself. Since no husband hates his own flesh, but nourishes and cherishes it, husbands should offer their wives the same concern and devotion they lavish on themselves.

Nourishing and Cherishing

In Ephesians 5:29, we are given the twin responsibilities of husbands. "Nourish" refers to taking care of our wives spiritually. The original Greek word is *ektrepho,* which means to nourish up to maturity, or to nurture. The word occurs only two times in Scripture, both in Paul's letter to the Ephesians. The other occurrence is in Ephesians 6:4: "Fathers, do not provoke your children to wrath, but bring them up (*ektrepho*) in the training and admonition of the Lord." It is interesting that each usage of *ektrepho* references how a husband should spiritually nourish the most important people in his life: his wife and children.

The second word, "cherish," denotes taking care of our wives physically, mentally, and emotionally. It refers to being tenderly affectionate, warm, and comforting. Husbands, let me ask you some questions that convict me when I ask them of myself.

- Are you as concerned about how your wife is doing as you are about how you are doing?
- Are you as concerned about how much sleep your wife is getting as about how much you are getting?
- When your wife is sick, are you as concerned about how she is doing as you are about yourself when you are sick?
- Are you as concerned about your wife's overworking herself as you are about overworking yourself?

If you love your wife as your own body, the answer to these questions will be, "Yes!"

We have ideas of what a husband should be willing to do for his wife, but God's ideas are very different from ours. We hope that any husband would be willing to jump in front of a car to save his wife. A husband has likely imagined someone breaking into his home and considered how he would protect his wife even at the cost of his own life. Yet when it comes to daily living, even heroic men are often less valiant in their willingness to lay aside their own agendas for the sake of their wives.

What does this look like practically? It looks like sacrifice. It means giving up things a husband would not have to give up if he did not have a wife. That could be sleep. Free time. Sports. Video games. Television. Time with friends. It means putting aside anything that prevents a husband from loving and caring for his wife the way he loves and cares for himself.

For some men, this means applying the words of 1 Corinthians 13:11: "When I was a child, I spoke as a child, I understood as a child, I thought as a child; but when I became a man, I put away childish things." Loving one's wife as God commands means putting away childish things. Another way to express this is: "I need to stop being a child. This is what boys do. I need to give this up and start being a man so I can love my wife as much as I love myself. It is time for me to 'man-up.'"

Chapter Ten

Protecting the Sanctity of Marriage

Ephesians 5:31—For this reason a man shall leave his
father and mother and be joined to his wife,
and the two shall become one flesh.

The apostle Paul quoted Genesis 2:24 in Ephesians 5:31, capturing God's divine plan for husbands and wives that He instituted at creation. The verse instructs husbands on the permanence of marriage and, again, Jesus is the standard. In John 10:28, He said regarding His future bride, the church: "And I give them eternal life, and they shall never perish; *neither shall anyone snatch them out of My hand.*"

Weddings are wonderful events because God divinely joins two separate individuals into one flesh. The Greek word for "joined" is *proskollao,* and it means "to glue upon." When a husband and wife are married, two separate halves are glued together creating one whole.

Paul's simple point is that marriage should never be broken or come apart. The one-flesh relationship God creates reveals why divorce is so terrible. When asked about divorce, Jesus quoted God's original command in Genesis 2:24, adding an even stronger injunction: "Therefore what God has joined together, *let not man separate*" (Matthew 19:6; Mark 10:9). Divorce tears apart what God Himself created.

How does God feel about people destroying what He has joined together? He hates it: "And let none deal treacherously with the wife of his youth. For *the LORD God of Israel says that He hates divorce,* for it covers one's garment with violence" (Malachi 2:15–16). These are strong words that equate divorce with violence. And why is that? Because divorce is the tearing apart of one flesh into two. God's hatred of divorce conveys two responsibilities to professing Christians:

1. No matter how difficult it might be—and it is difficult when we see people struggling in their marriage—believers have a responsibility to encourage others to stay married. While separation can and should be supported under certain circumstances, divorce should always be discouraged. When God says that He hates something, how can believers think of supporting it? Christians have the responsibility to help "what God has joined together" to stay together.

2. Christians cannot use the word "divorce" in their own marriages. Once this word is spoken, even if it is forgiven, it is often not forgotten. My wife and I counseled a couple who could not trust each other because both had used the "D" word. Each was convinced the other said it first, but that did not really matter because each had said it. Neither could forget what the other threatened, leaving husband and wife with little confidence in the other's commitment.

A divorce is like taking two pieces of metal that have been welded—or joined—together and ripping them apart. It is never going to be a nice split. Both pieces of metal are going to be damaged, and take some of the other piece with them. I am not trying to condemn those who have experienced a divorce (and the vast majority of people who have experienced the tragedy of divorce would confirm what I am saying here), but I am trying to encourage married couples never to consider divorce as an option. My hope is to spare families, especially those with children, the heartache divorce brings. My experience has been that most who have been through a divorce are the first to encourage pastors to preach more strongly against it. They want to see others avoid the same grief they have suffered.

Keep the Marriage in the Marriage

Before I begin this discussion, let me be clear: In cases of abuse, I am not suggesting that people cannot go to their parents (or others) for help.[13] With that said, when Paul commands "a man [to] leave his father and mother and be joined to his wife," he is in effect encouraging couples to keep the marriage between the husband and wife. Married individuals should cling to their spouses instead of their parents. When couples experience conflict, as all couples will, they should work things out together instead of running to parents for support.

This looks to the reason in-laws can contribute to the difficulties experienced in the marriage relationship, especially with newlyweds. I remember the story of a father who loved his daughter enough to send her back to her husband after the two had an argument. The father made it clear to his daughter that her husband was now the man in her life and thus she could not turn to him when she was upset.

This issue does not arise only with parents. When couples are experiencing conflict, they are tempted to go to others to criticize their spouses or gossip about how badly they are being treated. The obvious reason we want to do this is that we expect those close to us to side with us. Some wives turn to their girlfriends. Some husbands talk to their guy friends. While parents are specifically mentioned in the verse Paul quotes, a more encompassing principle here is that if we should not complain to our parents about our spouses, we should not complain to anyone else either.

The dangers here should be equally obvious. Pouring out our anger is simply going to stoke it. This will make us feel justified in responding poorly, as well as feed our belief that we deserve better treatment than we are receiving. It will make an already strained relationship worse.

---

[13] Chapter 13 discusses in more detail the appropriate responses to abuse.

An even worse scenario is when the offended party shares the grievances with someone of the opposite sex. The result will be:

- A wife's thinking: "I wish my husband listened to me the way so-and-so listens to me. I bet he would never treat me the way my husband treats me."
- A husband's thinking: "I bet so-and-so would show me more respect than my wife shows me. She would appreciate me and all of my hard work."

Complaining about your spouse to others is sinful and detrimental to the marriage. Ephesians 5:31 teaches us clearly that we are meant to keep our marriage in the marriage.

Seeking Godly Counsel Is the Exception

One exception to the rule of not going outside the marriage is when husbands and wives are seeking godly counsel. Couples who are having problems commonly make one of two mistakes:

1. They do not want to admit they are having problems and thus pretend everything is okay. They want to believe the problems will go away on their own. They want to keep their struggles a secret. As a result, they do not get help and their marriage worsens. This is one time the marriage should not stay in the marriage. Troubled couples should seek help outside the relationship.

2. They act as though they are seeking godly counsel when in fact they are only looking for the opportunity to gossip about their spouses. People committing this sin say, "I am having problems in my marriage and would like some advice." They then proceed to list everything bad their spouses have ever done without actually receiving counsel. Nor do they take any responsibility themselves. They do not share any of their own weaknesses or failures. They never say: "Please tell me what I did wrong. What do you think I should have done differently? How could I be a better spouse?"

These people are not looking for godly advice. They are just looking for an opportunity to complain and slander.

Unfortunately, those who want to badmouth their spouses will not have much trouble finding someone who will listen. Some people are all too eager to hear the denigrating information that should remain private. If you want counsel, do not seek out ungodly, immature friends who are more concerned about maintaining your friendship than helping your marriage. Many of these "friends" will poison a husband or wife against the spouse—and in doing so they are sinning against God. Typical responses from such people sound like:

- "I can't believe your wife did that. You should be mad!"
- "Your husband doesn't know what he has in you. You don't have to put up with that. You deserve so much better than him."

Instead of speaking to people who will provide counsel such as this, be willing to receive criticism and hear what you need to change. Seek out godly friends who love you and care about your marriage. Desire counsel that might sound like this:

- "Scripture commands you to love your wife. Encourage her and ask for forgiveness for the way you acted."
- "God says you should respect your husband. Stop talking to him like he is a child."

If you take the marriage outside the marriage, seek out people who will offer hard truths such as these.

The Bride's Supremacy

In Ephesians 5:31 the words "a man shall leave his father and mother and be joined to his wife" are a profound command that should deeply challenge husbands. They communicate a truth about the wife's importance in a man's life. To appreciate the significance of the verse, we need some familiarity with the marriage customs of the day to see just how much they differed from Paul's words.

A Jewish betrothal typically lasted one full year. During that time, the groom's main responsibility was to prepare a place for himself and his bride. He would then return at some unexpected time for his bride and take her to be with him at the place he prepared. For those acquainted with Jesus's own promise to His future bride in John 14:1–3, this should all sound familiar:

> Let not your heart be troubled; you believe in God, believe also in Me. In My Father's house are many mansions; if it were not so, I would have told you. I go to prepare a place for you. And if I go and prepare a place for you, I will come again and receive you to Myself; that where I am, there you may be also.

Jesus said He was going to prepare a place for His bride, the church. Where is that place? His Father's house. A Jewish groom would prepare a place for himself and his bride on his father's property. The newly established residence might even be attached to the father's house. This kept the newly married couple under the groom's parents' authority.

With this custom in mind, Paul's instruction in Ephesians 5 that a man should leave his father and mother could not have sounded more radical to the culture of the day. But as we have already seen, Paul was not saying something new here. He was, in fact, quoting Genesis 2:24, one of the earliest verses in Scripture. Paul was reiterating the divine plan for marriage to reestablish what God had instituted at creation.

Even though a man's father and mother have been the most important earthly relationship in his life up to his wedding day, a husband is commanded to "leave" them to be joined to his new bride. This means if a husband is to leave his parents for the sake of his wife, there is nothing he should not be willing to forsake for her. Second to a husband's relationship with Christ, his wife must be the supreme relationship in his life. A wife should never feel threatened by anyone or anything. A husband should have no earthly relationship that is more important than his relationship with his bride.

Perception Is Reality

Let me be clear. When wives feel like second place, it is not usually because of another woman. More often women feel like second place to some activity or hobby that takes priority in their husbands' lives. It could be sports, television, cars, poker night, alcohol, friends, work, video games, education, and even children. Yes, a husband's relationship with his wife should be supreme even above his relationship with his children. I love my children more than I can express in words, but I still try to let them know—and more importantly, let Katie know—that I love Mommy the most. For me, this means when I come home from work, I try to kiss and hug Katie before I kiss and hug my kids. I try to make sure Katie never feels as though she is competing with our children.

Note the emphasis here is how a wife *feels*. A husband might insist: "My wife is the supreme relationship in my life. She is more important than anything else." But the wife might not feel that way. A wife's perception is her reality. It is not about what the husband says or even thinks but about what the wife feels.

I will be the first to admit that I have not always been successful in this area. Let me share a personal story from early in my marriage that I still hate thinking of, much less writing about in a book. It is humbling, but through it I learned a lot, and I hope it might be instructive for you too. I was an elementary school teacher at the time, and I always tried to teach summer school. One summer the opportunity was not available and I came up with the terrible idea to play World of Warcraft, an online video game. Pretty quickly I found myself addicted.

At one point, I remember Katie expressing surprise at what I was doing. She was not angry or threatening, but I could tell she was disappointed and losing respect for me.

Then something life-changing happened. Our first child, Rhea, was born in July. About one week later, Katie had a breakdown. It was difficult for her to see me like this as her husband, but it was even worse for her when I was a father. She said she was afraid for our future and how this would affect our kids.

I repented, and by God's grace I immediately stopped playing. I thought it would be difficult to quit, but it was actually very easy. It felt like a huge weight had been lifted off my shoulders. I no longer felt like a slave, and the strong condemnation and shame were gone. There was peace in my relationship with the Lord, and I could pray and read the Word again without terrible conviction. Katie told me she was proud of me and that it was easy to respect me again.

Gentlemen, let me address you directly. I share this in the hope and prayer that, if you are reading these words and have something in your life that you cannot imagine getting rid of, you too might be given confidence to humble yourself before the Lord. Repent this very minute. Do not put it off. If you do this, you can experience the same freedom I experienced from bondage, shame, and losing your wife's respect. The conviction that constantly plagues your relationship with Christ will be gone too.

Before I finish here, let me be clear that I am not suggesting that husbands must categorically give up all hobbies they enjoy. For example, one husband might love restoring old cars, but does it only a few hours per month. His wife does not mind, so for him it is not a problem. Another husband spends every spare hour with his car. He is obsessed with it. His wife hates it. She resents him because of it. They cannot even talk about it without fighting. For him the car is a problem.

Too often in counseling, I have witnessed a wife's pain associated with some area of her husband's life. The husband says: "You're right. I'm sorry. I'll get my priorities in order. I'll make sure things are in balance. I'll make sure to do this in moderation." The husband will start off well. His wife will be happy for a few weeks. But slowly, whatever made the wife feel like second place will creep back into the husband's life, reclaiming that position of supremacy.

What is the solution? The solution is for the husband to remove the threat from his life completely. Put his wife in her rightful place. Make her the supreme relationship in his life. Jesus put it this way: "If your right eye causes you to sin, pluck it out and cast it from you . . . And if your right hand causes you to sin, cut it off and cast it from you" (Matthew 5:29–30, 18:8–9). We have to be ruthless with sin. If something in a husband's life is making his wife feel as though she is second place, then it is sin and he must take immediate action to remove it.

What is the reward when a husband obeys God's command to make his wife his greatest priority, second only to God Himself? The husband will enjoy the blessing of a prosperous and harmonious marriage and a happy and contented wife. He will enjoy having his wife's respect, and if there are children, he will gain their respect, too. A husband can enjoy a wife who has witnessed his sacrifice and can appreciate what he was willing to do for her and his family.

An Important Note for Wives

If you see your husband give something up so you can be the supreme relationship in his life, be sure to encourage him. Show him respect. Communicate how much you appreciate the sacrifice he is making for you and your family. Let him know that you are aware that few husbands love their wives and the Lord enough to do what he is doing.

The Greatest "Leaving and Cleaving"

Let me clarify that the command to "leave and cleave" is not encouraging children to cut their mother and father out of their lives. The phrase is referring to priorities. Both husbands and wives must make sure their spouses are more important than even their parents. This is what Jesus also wants from His bride, the church. In Matthew 10:37a He stated: "He who loves father or mother more than Me is not worthy of Me."

The most important "leaving and cleaving" we do in marriage is leaving the world and cleaving to Christ. When we place our own Bridegroom and Head first in our lives, we are actually strengthening our marriages because only in loving Christ and committing ourselves to Him can we become the husbands and wives God's Word commands us to be.

C. S. Lewis put it this way: "When I have learned to love God better than my earthly dearest, I shall love my earthly dearest better than I do now. When first things are put first, second things are not suppressed but increased."[14] Having a deep and sincere love for Christ is the best way to have a deep and sincere love for our spouses.

---

[14] C.S. Lewis, *The Collected Letters of C.S. Lewis, Volume 3: Narnia, Cambridge, and Joy 1950–1963* (HarperOne, 2007), p. 1952.

Chapter Eleven

A Wife Should
Respect Her Husband

*Ephesians 5:33—Nevertheless let each one of you
in particular so love his own wife as himself,
and let the wife see that she respects her husband.*

In Ephesians 5:25–32, the apostle Paul described in detail what it means for a husband to love his wife as himself. One might then expect the passage to end with similar instructions to the wife: "Let each one of you in particular *love his own wife* as himself, and let the wife *love her own husband* as herself." Instead, Paul commanded wives to *respect* their husbands.

This is not to say that men do not want to be loved. When we discussed *phileo* earlier, we reviewed the command in Titus 2:3–4: "Older women . . . admonish the young women to *love their husbands.*" I am also not saying that wives do not want to be respected. First Peter 3:7 says, "Husbands, likewise, dwell with [your wives] with understanding, giving honor to [them]." Honor is synonymous with respect. In fact, the NIV translates 1 Peter 3:7 as "treat them with respect." Thus, it is important for wives to be respected, and it is important for husbands to be loved.

But of the two—love and respect—respect is more important to husbands, and love is more important to wives:

- Husbands want to be loved, but they want to be respected even more.
- Wives want to be respected, but they want to be loved even more.

Consider how most wives covet their husbands' expressions of love, such as cards, phone calls, e-mails, or flowers. Though husbands might appreciate such gestures, what they desire more is their wives' respect. I do not need my wife to buy me flowers, call me during the day and tell me she loves me, or write me poetry. I might appreciate these things, but what I need is her respect.

In marriage counseling, when I hear wives expressing their frustrations about their husbands, it typically sounds like this: "I don't feel that my husband loves me. I wish my husband loved me more. He never tells me he loves me." But when husbands express frustration, it more often sounds like this: "I wish my wife respected me more. I wish my wife followed my lead. I wish my wife supported my decisions."

In truth, it is much easier for a wife to say she loves her husband than to show it through respect. But it is through respect that a wife expresses her love for her husband. If a wife does not show respect, her husband will not feel loved. A good perspective for couples to keep in mind is that feeling unloved is as painful to a wife as feeling disrespected is to a husband.

Modern research supports biblical instruction on this topic. Marriage expert Dr. Emerson Eggerichs shares some interesting statistics about husbands and wives in his well-known book, *Love and Respect*. In one survey, four hundred men were asked: "If you were forced to choose, would you prefer to feel alone and unloved or disrespected and inadequate?" Seventy-four percent responded that they would rather feel alone and unloved than disrespected and inadequate.

When Dr. Eggerichs conducted the same survey with women, a similar percentage of women responded that they would rather feel disrespected and inadequate than alone and unloved. Dr. Eggerichs sums up his findings: "[A wife] needs love just as she needs air to breathe, [and a husband] needs respect just as he needs air to breathe."

Another survey asked seven thousand people: "When you are in a conflict with your spouse, do you feel unloved or disrespected?" Eighty-three percent of husbands responded with "disrespected." Seventy-two percent of wives responded with "unloved."[15] This reveals that during marriage conflicts husbands often react because they feel disrespected and wives often react because they feel unloved.

What Respect Looks Like to a Husband

How does a wife convey respect to her husband? Here is a basic checklist of what respect looks like to a man.

Admiration—a wife respects her husband by admiring him, looking up to him, and holding him in high regard. In the Amplified Bible, Ephesians 5:33 reads:

> Let the wife see that she respects and reverences her husband [that she notices him, regards him, honors him, prefers him, venerates, and esteems him; and that she defers to him, praises him, and loves and admires him exceedingly].

Trustworthiness—Proverbs 31:11 says of the Virtuous Wife, "The heart of her husband safely trusts her." A husband feels respected when he can trust his wife. When he is away, she acts in a way that would please him just as though he were present. He is sure that she will not hide anything from him. Conversely, when a wife is untrustworthy, she communicates that she does not respect her husband's headship.

Protectiveness—a wife respects her husband by protecting his name and reputation. She does not slander him or complain about him behind his back. With the prevalence of social media, a wife's criticism of her husband can be much more damaging than when she gossips to her friends. With a single click of the mouse, hundreds of people can become aware of the wife's accusations against her husband.

Proverbs 31:23 says of the Virtuous Wife, "Her husband is [respected] in the gates when he sits among the elders of the land." Why is there a verse praising a husband in a passage that is all about his wife? How is his

---

[15] Dr. Emerson and Sarah Eggerichs. "About Us." Love & Respect Ministries. 2016. Accessed March 7, 2016. http://loveandrespect.com/about-us/.

position a credit to her? This husband would not be respected and sitting among the elders if he had a wife whose behavior or speech caused others to lose respect for him. There are husbands who will never achieve leadership positions in their church or community because of the way their wives demean them or damage their reputation behind their backs.

Appreciation—a wife respects her husband by expressing appreciation of how hard he works to care for his family and by considering the sacrifices he makes to be a good father and husband. Few attitudes communicate respect more than thankfulness, and few attitudes communicate disrespect more than ingratitude. And this leads us to the next section.

What Disrespect Looks Like to a Husband

Conversely, no matter how much a wife might profess her love, certain attitudes communicate disrespect to her husband.

Discontentment—when a wife routinely expresses frustration with her life, her home, her family, or her possessions, she is disrespecting her husband. A discontented wife makes her husband feel like a failure because he is the one—at least in her eyes—who is not providing well enough.

Disparaging speech and body language—a wife disrespects her husband when she:

- Talks down to him or treats him like a little boy who is in trouble
- Interrupts him or talks over him
- Rolls her eyes, huffs and puffs, or wags her finger at him

Even worse is when such disparaging speech and actions extend to others, such as telling friends "a funny story" about a husband's inability to do something or how many times it took him to fix something.

Second-guessing—even when a wife is doing her best to respect her husband, she sends the opposite message when she second-guesses everything he says, offers all the reasons he is wrong, constantly corrects him, or undermines him when he makes a decision. The wife might be trying to be helpful, but her actions communicate: "I do not trust you. You don't know what you are doing. I could do this better." Sometimes the words, "I'm just trying to help," do not help.

Badmouthing Dad to the kids—a wife terribly disrespects her husband when she belittles him in front of their children. There is absolutely nothing wrong with a wife disagreeing with her husband, but there is a right and a wrong way for wives to handle such feelings. Disagreements between a husband and wife should be carried out in private. When a wife corrects her husband in front of their children, she destroys his credibility with them. Instead, a wife should strive to build up her children's good opinion of their father.

As a wife looks for her husband's best qualities, focuses on her husband's strengths, speaks well of him to others, and praises him to their children, she will find her respect for her husband growing. Conversely, if she speaks badly about her husband to others—whether they be friends, neighbors, or the children—she will find her respect for her husband diminishing.

Learning Your Husband's Respect Gauge

After listening to hundreds of hours of my teaching, Katie often knows how I will answer questions and can even finish sentences for me. Because of this familiarity she can help me know when not to say certain things. She will swipe her hand across the front of her neck, signaling, "Not a good idea." Perhaps the most common criticism I have received of my preaching is that I talk too quickly. Katie will make a hand motion that lets me know to slow down.

I find these actions helpful, but Katie has had other women tell her: "I can't imagine doing that to my husband when he is talking." I have had men ask me: "You don't mind when your wife does that?"

At the same time, there are things other men might find helpful that Katie knows I find disrespectful. This is why it is so important for wives to learn their husbands. We will talk more about submission in Part V, but for now it is important to note that the biblical instruction for wives to submit to their husbands also includes the concept of adapting. This is captured in the Amplified Bible:

- Ephesians 5:22—Wives, be subject [be submissive and *adapt* yourselves] to your own husbands as [a service] to the Lord.
- Colossians 3:18—Wives, be subject to your husbands [subordinate and adapt yourselves to them], as is right and fitting and your proper duty in the Lord.
- Titus 2:5a—[Wives should] be self-controlled, chaste, homemakers, good-natured [kindhearted], adapting and subordinating themselves to their husbands.
- 1 Peter 3:1a—In like manner, you married women, be submissive to your own husbands [subordinate yourselves as being secondary to and dependent on them, and *adapt* yourselves to them].

Learning, Then Embracing

How does a wife adapt to her husband? By learning what is important to him and making it important to her.

- Is your husband punctual? Work hard to be on time.
- Does he have to be up early and thus wants to be in bed by a certain time? Strive to be in bed by that time.
- Does it bother him when certain things are messy or left out? Try to make sure these areas are tidy.

As my wife once shared at a woman's event: "Ladies, work hard to make your husband's priorities your own and to put your priorities second. And when you adapt to him, do not make him feel stupid for the way he wants things done."

Since husbands are called to be spiritual leaders, one of the best ways a wife can respect her husband is by embracing his vision for the family and doing what she can to see it fulfilled. She passes along his ideas and desires to the children. A wife who does this will have a husband who feels very respected.

An interesting parallel to this in the military is the relationship between a platoon leader and platoon sergeant. Typically, a platoon leader is a brand-new junior officer. In contrast, the platoon sergeant may be a career soldier far more knowledgeable in many areas. Regardless, the platoon leader is the commanding officer responsible for developing the orders and vision for the platoon. The sergeant's responsibility is to embrace the platoon leader's plans and see that they are carried out. The relationship between leader and sergeant is not based on who is wiser or more experienced but on the chain of command. Still, a smart platoon leader will recognize his platoon sergeant's experience and wisdom and seek his thoughts and counsel.

Similarly, a wife may have more experience and wisdom in some areas than her husband, but God has still appointed the husband to be the head and He expects the wife to embrace his leadership. A husband should recognize his wife's wisdom and experience and seek her thoughts in making decisions and establishing the vision for the family.[16]

A Portrait of Love Without Respect

Plenty of men are walking around feeling loved by their wives but not respected by them. Scripture provides a perfect picture of a woman who loved her husband without respecting him: Saul's daughter, Michal, the first wife of King David. Even though she was responsible for one of the strongest displays of disrespect ever recorded from a wife toward a husband, Michal is also the only woman Scripture specifically mentions as loving her husband: 1 Samuel 18:20 says, "Michal, Saul's daughter, loved David."

This is not to say other women in Scripture did not love their husbands. I am sure many of them did—but it is not emphasized. Why is that? I admit I am being a little speculative here. Perhaps it is because—as we have already discussed—the priority is for women to respect their

---

[16] Read more about this in Chapter 13.

husbands rather than to love them. As a result, Scripture emphasizes a wife's respect more than her love. Abraham's wife, Sarah, is a case in point. We will examine her biography in Chapter 17, but for now it is worth noticing that she is held up as an example for wives, not because of her love but because of her submission and respect.

This also reveals why Michal, even though she is the one wife in Scripture said to love her husband, is not praised. The disrespect she showed David ruined any potential of her being a positive example for women. We find her conduct toward David in 2 Samuel 6.

Soon after David became king of the nation of Israel, one of his top priorities was transporting the ark of the covenant to his capital. The biblical account describes this as one of the most joyful moments of the new king's life. As the procession entered Jerusalem, "David danced before the LORD with all his might" (2 Samuel 6:14). Unfortunately, Michal did not share her husband's joy. In 2 Samuel 6:16 we read: "Michal, Saul's daughter, looked through a window and saw King David leaping and whirling before the LORD; and she despised him in her heart."

Michal thought David's behavior was terribly unbecoming. Her father, Saul, was all about appearances, and he would never act this way. Perhaps this had rubbed off on Michal, so she found David's behavior far below the dignity of a king. Second Samuel 6:20 records her reaction:

> Then David returned to bless his household. And Michal the daughter of Saul came out to meet David, and said, "How glorious was the king of Israel today, uncovering himself today in the eyes of the maids of his servants, as one of the base fellows shamelessly uncovers himself!"

King David arrived home eager to share his joy with his family, but Michal was so disgusted with him that she could not even wait until he got inside. Picture a mother coming out to reprimand a child. You can hear the scorn and disrespect in her words. Wives might ask themselves: "Am I like this? Do I pounce on my husband when he does something wrong? Do I ridicule him over something inconsequential? Do I make him feel like a little boy who is in trouble?"

Just to be clear, Michal was not the only one wrong in this situation. David did not respond lovingly to his wife. Second Samuel 6:21–22 records:

> So David said to Michal, "It was before the LORD, who chose me instead of your father and all his house, to appoint me ruler over the people of the Lord, over Israel. Therefore I will play music before the LORD. And I will be even more undignified than this, and will be humble in my own sight. But as for the maidservants of whom you have spoken, by them I will be held in honor."

David harshly pointed out that God chose him over Michal's father and then added: "You think this is bad? I'll act even worse than this!" The phrase "held in honor" may be the clearest and simplest definition of respect in the Bible. David told Michal: "You might not respect me, but there are plenty of other women who do." Pointing out other women's feelings was prideful and insensitive.

Disrespect Can Change a Husband's Feelings Toward His Wife

This encounter between David and Michal does not end happily: "Therefore Michal the daughter of Saul had no children to the day of her death" (2 Samuel 6:23). I take this to mean that David no longer had sexual relations with Michal. I am not defending David's actions. We discussed how husbands are supposed to love their wives unconditionally, and David definitely did not do that. As is the case in most marriage conflicts, both spouses were at fault:

- It is sinful for husbands to punish their wives as David punished Michal.
- It is sinful for wives to disrespect their husbands as Michal disrespected David.

With that said, it is important to notice how dramatically this one event changed David's relationship with Michal. Only a few chapters earlier, he made every effort to be reunited with his wife (2 Samuel 3:13–14). This reveals how much David previously longed to be with Michal. But once Michal disrespected David so drastically, his attitude toward her changed drastically. He now resented her. It was not the right response, but it was the reality.

It is no different today. When husbands are strongly disrespected by their wives, they become resentful and distance themselves from them. It is not right, but it is a common fruit of disrespect. If not dealt with, the result may be a destroyed relationship such as that between David and Michal.

It Is Not an Option for Husbands or Wives

The account between David and Michal is very instructive:

- It gives wives an example of how not to treat their husbands.
- It gives husbands an example of how not to respond to their wives.
- It illustrates that wives loving their husbands is not the same as respecting them. Perhaps Michal still loved David at this point, but we can be sure that he did not feel loved because of the way she disrespected him.

In the previous chapter, we discussed how a wife must feel supreme. It is not about what the husband thinks or says but about how the wife *feels*. Similarly, a husband must feel respected. It is not about what the wife thinks or says but about how the husband *feels*. Just as a wife's perception regarding being the supreme relationship in her husband's life is her reality, so too is a husband's perception regarding being respected his reality.

Additionally, we discussed how husbands are commanded to love their wives even when they do not feel like it. The same is true for wives. Ephesians 5:33 says, "Let the wife see that she respects her husband" without containing the word "if." Just as husbands are to love their wives when they do not feel like it, wives are to respect their husbands when they do not feel like it. As much as wives want their husbands to love them unconditionally, husbands want their wives to respect them unconditionally.

The moment any marriage becomes conditional with a husband saying, "I am not going to love my wife because she . . ." or a wife saying, "I am not going to respect my husband because he . . ." the marriage suffers. When each spouse's obedience is not conditional on his or her love for Christ but rather on the other spouse's behavior, this is the recipe for a miserable marriage. Only when two people are equally committed to obeying God's commands unconditionally will a marriage experience the health and joy God desires for it.

Making Loving and Respecting Easier

Even though a husband is commanded to love his wife, a wife can make loving her easier. Some wives are definitely more *lovable* than others. Some husbands reading this have been saying, "I want to love my wife, but if you only had any idea of the way she acts!" Ladies, make it easier for your husband to obey God's commands!

Similarly, even though a wife is commanded to respect her husband, a husband can make respecting him easier. I shared how difficult it was for Katie to respect me when I was playing World of Warcraft. Some wives reading this have been saying, "I want to look up to my husband . . ." but they find it difficult because their husband does not work hard to take care of his family, mistreats their children, or looks at things he should rip his eyes away from. Part of being a loving husband is also being a husband who seeks to earn his wife's respect. Husbands, make it easier for your wife to obey God's commands!

Part V:

Understanding Submission

Chapter Twelve

Equal Opportunity Submission

Ephesians 5:21—Submitting to
one another in the fear of God.

I f you are an American, I have bad news for you. You may have more
trouble with submission than most people. Submission is considered
not only un-American but downright anti-American. "Give me liberty or
give me death," was Founding Father Patrick Henry's famous declaration
during the American Revolution. And, indeed, Americans value liberty
more than almost anything else. Certainly, to many people, submission
looks like a loss of liberty. We might paraphrase "Give me liberty or give
me death!" as "I'd rather die than submit!"

A nation that prides itself on a notion such as this will view submission
negatively, and there are two problems for Christians who also find
themselves in this category:

1. The Bible speaks frequently of submission, so if you have a
   problem with submission you will have a problem with much of
   the Bible.

2. Submission—or having a submissive spirit—is spoken of
   positively. If you do not want to be a submissive person, you are
   going to have a hard time following Christ.

Submission Is Not Only for Wives

Often when we hear the word "submission" the first thing that comes to mind is God's command for wives to submit to their husbands. But wives are far from the only believers commanded to submit; every Christian is called to submit in a number of ways. Later we will examine 1 Peter 3:1–6, an in-depth passage commanding wives to submit to their husbands, but before Peter instructs wives he first discusses submission in a number of other relationships:

- 1 Peter 2:13–17 commands believers to submit to government (see also Romans 13:1–7).
- 1 Peter 2:18–25 commands slaves to submit to their masters; in our society this would translate as employees' submitting to employers (see also Ephesians 6:5–8).
- 1 Peter 5:5 commands congregations to submit to their elders (see also Hebrews 13:17).

Additionally, in Ephesians 6:1, the apostle Paul commands children to submit to their parents (see also Colossians 3:20). He also instructs wives to submit to their husbands in Ephesians 5:22, but one verse earlier, in Ephesians 5:21, he commands believers to submit to one another. This calls us to have a submissive spirit that is willing to give up rights and wishes for the sake of unity in the body of Christ. We see this described more clearly in Philippians 2:3–4:

> Let nothing be done through selfish ambition or conceit, but in lowliness of mind let each esteem others better than himself. Let each of you look out not only for his own interests, but also for the interests of others.

Our spiritual liberty is not only about freedom but equally about giving up—i.e., submitting—our rights for others. If a brother or sister in Christ would be offended or stumble on account of one of our liberties, we submit to that person by laying down our rights (Romans 14:14–23; 1 Corinthians 8:9–13). Paul says in Romans 12:18: "If it is possible, as much as depends on you, live peaceably with all men." Hebrews 12:14 reiterates: "Pursue peace with all people." Establishing this peace, whether in the marriage relationship or any other relationship, involves submission. It involves making sacrifices in deference to others.

The Way We Submit Is as Important as Submitting

When I taught elementary school, I told students on the first day that the way they did what I asked was as important as doing what I asked. For example:

- If I instructed a student to take out a book, and the student slammed it defiantly on his desk, he would be in as much trouble as if he had not taken out the book at all.
- If I told a student to push in her chair, but she pushed it in while rolling her eyes, she would be in as much trouble as if she had not pushed in the chair at all.

The way we submit—whether students to teachers, children to parents, congregations to elders, believers to government, employees to employers, believers to one another, or wives to husbands—is as important as submitting itself. If we submit with a bad attitude, we are not really submitting. We may think of submission as an outward action, but it is something we do inwardly. Submission is an issue of the heart.

One interesting note about the Greek word for "submit"—*hypotasso*—is that it is actually a military term meaning "to arrange [troop divisions] in a military fashion under the command of a leader." It reminds me of a lesson I will never forget from my time in the United States Army. A superior officer asked those of us under his command: "What do you do with every command you receive?"

We gave any number of answers:

- "Make sure you know exactly what you are being asked to do."
- "Learn from the order."
- "Carry out the request as quickly as possible."

Nobody had the right response. Finally, we were told: "Take the order and make it your own."

What he meant was any time we are given a command, we should do it as though we want to do it. If a soldier moaned, groaned, rolled his eyes, complained, or argued with his commander when asked to do something, he would be considered insubordinate. To say it would be frowned upon is an understatement. Likewise, we should recognize how much it is spiritually frowned upon if we do that when submitting. This can apply to:

- Students when they submit to their teachers
- Children when they submit to their parents
- Employees when they submit to their bosses
- Wives when they submit to their husbands

And this applies to husbands when they do things for their wives. Will it really bless a wife if a husband sighs and complains while changing a diaper or washing the dishes?

Obey the Bible, Not the World

These days we often hear about the "redefinition" of marriage. Such discussions typically refer to marriage as being something other than the union of one man and one woman for life. But there is another way society has redefined marriage, and that is in relation to the roles and responsibilities of husbands and wives. Consider this: Even non-Christian friends and neighbors have no issue discussing husbands' loving their wives, but mention male headship or submission, and you can count on facing fierce opposition. Here is what self-proclaimed feminist Cath Elliot said about biblical womanhood:

> Unfortunately, as in any movement for social change, there are those who remain resistant to their own [freedom]: a tiny minority of women who have been so indoctrinated by religious conditioning that they continue to see themselves as men's subordinates . . . Biblical womanhood does exactly what it says it does: it sends women back to the dark ages. At the [True Woman] Conference, for example, the Christian sisters launched their new

manifesto, inspiringly titled "The True Woman Manifesto," where they resolved to cultivate "such virtues as purity, modesty, submission, meekness, and love" and where they affirmed their calling as women "to encourage men as they seek to express godly masculinity, and to honor and support God-ordained male leadership in the home and in the church." It's encouraging to see that only three thousand women have signed this terrible charter, but it's also depressing to think that three thousand women think so little of themselves and their daughters that they're prepared to endorse such illiberal, anti-woman nonsense.[17]

Obviously, a radical feminist such as Ms. Elliot thinks submission enslaves women and ruins their lives. But she is not alone. This is the prevailing view of our society regarding the roles of husbands and wives. More tragic yet is the fact that this is even the view of some churches.

In support of the biblical view of submission, Dr. Jay Adams, founder of the Institute for Nouthetic Studies (INS), the National Association of Nouthetic Counselors (NANC), and the Christian Counseling and Educational Foundation (CCEF) explained:

> Submission does not remove freedom; it allows for it. When is the train freer? When it is bumping over the hillside off the track? Or when it is smoothly running along the track, confined or restricted, if you will, to the track? It is freer when it is where it ought to be, doing what it was intended to do . . . Freedom in God's world never comes apart from structure. When one is free to live as God intended, he is truly free indeed. We hear much about women's liberation today. I want you to be liberated. Here is the path of genuine liberation for a woman: submission. Submission allows her to run on the track; it allows her to make beautiful music in her home.[18]

---

[17] Cath Elliot. "Beware the anti-feminists." The Guardian. January 28, 2009. Accessed March 7, 2016. http://www.theguardian.com/commentisfree/2009/jan/28/women-gender.

[18] Jay Adams, *Christian Living in the Home* (P&R, 1972), pp. 74–75.

Dr. Adams's point, which is equally true for husbands, is that true freedom is experienced when we live our lives in obedience to God. True freedom comes when we strive to be husbands and wives as God commanded rather than as society defines. Jesus said: "You shall know the truth, and the truth shall make you free" (John 8:32). This is why we need to embrace what Scripture says. Real freedom and joy—whether for young, old, male, female, single, or married—comes from obeying God. Disobedience always leads to frustration and bondage.

Whenever we read the Bible, we face two choices:

- We can shape Scripture to fit our desires and beliefs.
- We can allow Scripture to shape us and our thinking.

As Christians, we will undoubtedly say we want the latter, but the real difficulty is that we live in a world that is also striving to shape and influence us. This is why the apostle Paul said, "Do not be conformed to this world, but be transformed by the renewing of your mind, that you may prove what is that good and acceptable and perfect will of God" (Romans 12:2). Paul identified the world—that is, the view of the society that surrounds us—as a conforming influence on our lives, but he told us to have our minds transformed instead.

What does this mean? The Greek word for "conformed" is *syschematizo*, which means "to conform one's self—one's mind and character—to another's pattern . . . fashion one's self according to." It is related to the English word *schematic* because it is describing the way society tempts us to follow its patterns. Instead we are to be "transformed," which is *metamorphoo*, related to the English word *metamorphosis*. Picture a caterpillar bursting from its cocoon, transformed into a beautiful butterfly. Similarly, we are transformed in mind and character as we resist the world and surrender ourselves to God's Word.

Allowing our minds to be transformed in this way can be difficult, especially when we come across verses that are hard to accept or with which we disagree. When our beliefs are challenged, it is at those moments that we need to choose to submit to Scripture. Unless we think we are wiser than God, we need to trust that He knows best.

We may think "walking by faith" means going overseas as a missionary or taking on some ministry that is terrifying to us, but walking by faith plays out more often in our lives when we look at God's Word and say: "This does not make sense to me, but I am going to obey anyway." Before you read any further in the book, I hope you will make the decision to let the Bible transform your view of marriage. Otherwise, you will end up being conformed by the world. This is especially important when discussing submission since it is a doctrine so largely rejected within our society and, sadly, even within some churches.

The Need for Submission

An examination of basic leadership structures makes clear submission is an important principle in every area of human interaction. No organization can be successful without authority or headship:

- Businesses have CEOs.
- Sports teams have coaches.
- Governments have presidents or prime ministers.

Just as we recognize the need for a leader, or a head, we also recognize that there cannot be two heads. We do not see two head coaches, two presidents, two head pilots, or two head surgeons. Imagine how uncomfortable you would feel flying on a plane where two head pilots are arguing over the flight plan. Imagine being operated on by two head surgeons quarreling over the proper procedure. Instead we always see a head coach and an assistant coach, a president and a vice-president, a pilot and a co-pilot, a principal and an assistant principal. The second-in-command is expected to submit to the authority of the leader in charge.

Since we recognize the need for orderly leadership in all other areas of life we should recognize the same need in marriage and appreciate how clear God makes it in Scripture. Consider three points:

1. Wives are instructed five times in the New Testament to submit to their husbands (Ephesians 5:22, 5:24; Colossians 3:18; Titus 2:3–5; 1 Peter 3:1). The repetition makes this one of the most common commands in God's Word.

2. Every New Testament passage that discusses the marriage relationship commands wives to submit. A wife's role is inextricably linked to and contingent on her submission to her husband. God does not see wives' relationships to their husbands separately from their submission to their husbands.

3. Despite all the New Testament verses we have looked at instructing submission toward various individuals—employers, elders, government, parents, husbands—it is significant that there is no verse instructing husbands to submit to their wives.

Unfortunately, since Ephesians 5:21 says to "[submit] to one another," it is sometimes used to argue that husbands and wives should submit equally to each other. There are a few problems with that interpretation:

*   Ephesians 5:21 does not refer to the marriage relationship but is talking about believers' mutual responsibilities toward each other. Paul does not discuss marriage specifically until verse 22 when he begins addressing wives and husbands directly.

*   As we saw in Chapter 6, at least two husbands—Adam and Ahab—were rebuked for submitting to their wives (Genesis 3:17; 1 Kings 21:25).

*   Paul cannot be teaching that husbands should submit to their wives because that would conflict with instruction that immediately follows in verses 22 and 24 for wives to submit to their husbands, as well as similar instruction in Colossians 3:18, Titus 2:5, and 1 Peter 3:1.

Submission Is for When a Wife Disagrees

A wife is commanded to respect her husband and submit to him. Is there a difference between the two commands?

- Respect deals with a wife's feelings toward her husband and the way she treats him as a result.
- Submission deals with a wife's response to her husband when she disagrees with his decision.

One of the most common arguments I have heard from wives who do not want to submit to their husbands is: "I would submit to my husband if I agreed with him." Can we see the problem with this logic? If a wife agreed with her husband, she would not have to submit. Submission is in place entirely for when husbands and wives do not agree. Perhaps a husband and wife have discussed a decision together, presented their ideas, shared their thoughts, and tried to come to an agreement. But they cannot. At this point, what do they do? How do they decide? Do they flip a coin or play "Rock-Paper-Scissors"? Just as in all the authority structures we have discussed, there is a clear answer here, and it is an answer God has decreed, not man. For the marriage to be able to move forward, the husband has been designated to make the final decision.

Two points should be kept in mind regarding husbands and wives discussing decisions together:

1. Although it is ideal when a decision takes place only after a husband has given his wife ample time to share her thoughts, some situations might not allow for lengthy discussions. If for whatever reason, time is limited and a presentation of both sides and opinions is not feasible, wives are still expected to submit to their husbands.

2. As much as a husband should strive to hear his wife's thoughts, a wife should strive not to exasperate her husband. She should not say, "You can't make a decision yet, because you haven't heard everything I have to say," while presenting countless variations of the same opinion said in different ways.

When a wife has to submit, she needs to remember if her husband is wrong, he will be held responsible. The decision is on his shoulders. Her responsibility ends at submitting, not at making sure the right decision is made. Marriage expert and author Wayne Mack explains it this way:

> Submission means a wife sees herself as part of her husband's team. She has ideas, opinions, desires, requests, and insights, and she lovingly makes them known. But she knows that in any good team someone has to make the final decision. She knows the team members must support the team leader, his plans and decisions, or no progress will be made and confusion and frustration will result. Fifty-fifty marriages [where the husband leads half the time and the wife leads half the time] are an impossibility. They do not work. They cannot work. In marriage someone has to be the final decision maker, and God has ordained that this should be the husband."[19]

Submission is difficult. It is tough for men to lead spiritually, and it is just as tough for wives to submit. Wives should be encouraged by the reality that submission does not mean supporting the idea but supporting the man behind it. When wives submit, they should remember they are doing it out of love for God and their husbands.

A Husband Can Make Submission Easier, but He Can Never Make It Easy

We discussed how a husband can make respecting him easier, but making submitting to him easier is a different issue. Generally, a wife has trouble respecting her husband if there is sin in his life, but a wife often has trouble submitting to her husband if he is not a spiritual man. It is difficult for a wife to trust a man who does not pray, read the Bible, is not involved in the church, or does not seem to have a heart for God. The reason should be obvious. A wife will have little confidence in her husband's ability to make the right decisions for the family.

---

[19] Wayne Mack, *Strengthening You Marriage* (P&R, June 1, 1999), p. 14.

A woman wants a man who is guided by the Lord. When a wife knows her husband regularly spends time in prayer and in God's Word, she will have a much easier time placing her life and the lives of her children in his hands. She will feel confident in his judgment. There are plenty of reasons for a husband to pray and study Scripture regularly, and one of those reasons is so that his wife can say: "I trust my husband. He wants what the Lord wants. He is receptive to God's will. I know this because his spiritual life makes it obvious." Being a man of the Word and a man of prayer is the greatest way for a husband to make his wife's submission easier.

To bring some balance to this section though, you will notice that the subtitle speaks of husbands making submission *easier* instead of *easy*. This is because it will always be difficult for wives to submit to their husbands. God told Eve, "Your desire shall be for your husband" (Genesis 3:16). As we discussed earlier, this refers to a desire for women to control their husbands. It might help for a man to be loving and godly, but as a result of the curse, wives are going to struggle with submission regardless of what their husbands are or are not like.

While a wife might insist that she would submit to her husband if only he were more like Christ, this is not a valid argument because Christ loves all wives perfectly, and they still fall short of submitting perfectly to Him. In conclusion, husbands can make submission easier for their wives by being godly men, but as part of the curse, a wife will have trouble submitting even to the godliest man.

Chapter Thirteen

What Submission Does Not Mean

How far does submission extend? Is there anything to which a wife should not submit? Are all women required to submit to all men? Does submission mean men can do whatever they like to their wives? What about physical or mental abuse? In any discussion of submission, some obvious and legitimate questions arise. To answer them, let's look at what biblical submission does *not* mean.

Submission Does Not Mean
That Wives Submit to Other Men

While Scripture is clear that God commands wives to submit to their husbands, it is equally clear that wives are commanded to submit *only* to their husbands. Each command in Scripture for wives to submit makes this clear:

- Ephesians 5:22a—Wives, submit to your own husbands.
- Ephesians 5:24—Therefore, just as the church is subject to Christ, so let the wives be to their own husbands in everything.
- Colossians 3:18a—Wives, submit to your own husbands.
- Titus 2:3—5 Older women likewise . . . admonish the young women . . . to be obedient to their own husbands.
- 1 Peter 3:1a—Wives, likewise, be submissive to your own husbands.

Wives should see themselves under their own husbands' authority, but not under the authority of other husbands. Even in the church, a wife is under the authority of her husband, and her husband is under the authority of the leadership of the church: "the head of every man is Christ, the head of woman is man" (1 Corinthians 11:3).

In Genesis 2:18 when God spoke of creating the first woman, He did not say, "I will make men [plural] helpers." He said: "I will make *him* [singular] a helper." When I want help in my life, I most often look to my wife or other men God has put in my life, but I do not look to other men's wives because I know they are other men's helpers.

Practically, this also addresses the misconception that submission means women can only hold positions—in or out of the church—in which they are subordinate to all male associates. Such an extreme interpretation would suggest that a woman cannot be a nurse because a male orderly might be her subordinate or that a woman could not be a teacher because a male aide or janitor might help her at times.

Submission Does Not Mean That Wives Submit to Abuse

What women long for is spiritual and moral leadership from their husbands—not spiritual or moral domination. While this is fairly straightforward, it is still worth making some clarifications. When we hear the word "abuse," the next word that most likely comes to mind is "physical." Abuse, however, can be emotional, mental, or even spiritual as well. There are wives whose husbands never lay a hand on them but mistreat them so badly they are in worse condition than even physically abused women.

What should a woman in an abusive relationship do? She cannot divorce her husband, but she can separate from him. The apostle Paul writes: "If [a wife] does depart, let her remain unmarried or be reconciled to her husband. A wife is bound to her husband as long as he lives" (1 Corinthians 7:11, 39; Romans 7:2). If the abused woman is part of a church, elders or others should be willing to receive her (and possibly her children) while counseling is performed, repentance is sought, and the gospel is given time to work in the husband's heart. An abused wife may also need to seek social or legal services, a battered woman's shelter, and even the police, if the abuse warrants such.

That said, the abuse card can be used carelessly. I have heard women throw out the word "abuse" simply because their husbands do not treat them with sufficient adoration or give them everything they want. When a wife does not get to do all the things she wants to do, go all the places she wants to go, buy all the things she wants to buy, or spend all her time the way she wants to, that is not abuse.

Additionally, having a husband who is less than perfect does not constitute abuse. God commands husbands to love their wives as Christ loved the church. No husband does this perfectly. Husbands regularly sin against their wives, but this does not mean a husband is being abusive. If failing to love one's wife perfectly constituted abuse, then every wife on earth would be in an abusive relationship.

Submission Does Not Mean That Wives Submit to Sin

The account in Acts 5:1–11 of Ananias and his wife, Sapphira, is instructive. The background of this story is that early church members sold their possessions to share with the apostles and other needy believers. Ananias sold a possession, kept part of the money when he brought his offering to the apostles, but acted as though all of the proceeds were being given to the church. As the apostle Peter reminded him, Ananias had every right to keep part of his profits. It was Ananias's claim, however, to have turned over all the funds that resulted in his dropping dead on the spot for lying to the Holy Spirit.

The correlation is that Ananias "kept back part of the proceeds, *his wife also being aware of it*" (Acts 5:2). When Sapphira showed up, not realizing her husband had died, she had the opportunity to tell the truth. Instead, she reiterated her husband's lie, and Peter said, "How is it that *you have agreed together* to test the Spirit of the Lord? Look, the feet of those who have buried your husband are at the door, and they will carry you out" (Acts 5:9).

God's judgment on Sapphira for supporting her husband's sin shows she was as accountable as he was. If she had refused to participate in the deception, Peter's response indicates her life would have been spared. This event is a perfect example of a time when a wife should not have submitted to her husband.

Let me add a caveat that the principle in question applies to being asked to engage in blatant sin. A wife should say no to a husband who demands that she participate in drug dealing, theft, adultery, or even lesser offenses, such as cheating on income tax or lying to an employer. This is quite different from a husband opposing his wife's involvement in positive spiritual activities. A husband may resist his wife's taking time from home and family to join a Bible study fellowship, attend church several times a week, volunteer for a Christian outreach, or participate in a church sports league. He is not asking her to commit a sin but simply to respect his priorities. What is a wife supposed to do, especially when the activities can contribute to her spiritual growth?

A wife can respectfully let her husband know her desires and ask if he would allow this for the benefit of their marriage, children, or family. If he is still resistant, then she should submit and pray that God will change his heart. Assuming God wants the family involved in the particular activity, that is something He can easily do. Even if she does not like her husband's decision, she should be encouraged that God will reward her submission and—assuming the husband is disobeying God by declining—hold the husband responsible for his poor spiritual leadership.

Submission Does Not Mean That Husbands Do Not Defer to Their Wives

Every healthy, joyful marriage in which a woman feels loved is a marriage in which a husband defers to his wife. Godly men are not going to throw submission around loosely. They will first strive to reach an agreement with their wives. Even when an agreement cannot be reached, especially when the issue is not crucial, they may still choose to defer to their wives.

Let me share an example from my marriage. Not long ago I decided a great plan would be to surprise the family with one of my favorite foods—popcorn—and a show filled with thrills, tremendous plot lines, and edge-of-your-seat action—*Little House on the Prairie*. While I was working up an appetite doing cardio, my mom called to say: "Katie invited us to go out for frozen yogurt with all of you. When do you want us to come over?"

Now I am sure many husbands can relate to this. You are excited about some way you would like to spend your evening only to find out that your wife wants to do something else. My first thought was that Katie and I had not discussed getting frozen yogurt. My second thought was that the frozen yogurt shop did not sell popcorn or show *Little House on the Prairie*.

At that moment I had two choices. I could put my foot down and say: "I've already decided we are going to have popcorn and watch *Little House on the Prairie*, so that is what we're going to do." Or I could decide: "You know what? I'm going to sacrifice for my wife. I'm going to pick up my cross . . . and take it to the frozen yogurt shop."

This might seem like a trivial example, but the point I am trying to make is that even though wives are commanded to submit to their husbands, godly husbands look for ways to bless their wives, even when it is not what the husbands want. Ephesians 5:26 says husbands ought to love their wives as their own bodies, and apparently my wife's body wanted frozen yogurt. You can guess where we ended up, and, no, it did not include popcorn or *Little House on the Prairie*.

Submission Does Not Mean That Husbands Do Not Listen to Their Wives

We have already learned how God created the woman to give man a "helper comparable to him" (Genesis 2:18). I do not want to sound too simplistic, but in my mind, the three greatest resources God has given a husband on this side of heaven are:

1. The Word of God
2. The Holy Spirit (also called "the Helper")
3. His wife

A husband who does not listen to his wife is forfeiting one of the greatest resources God has given him. Additionally, consider how these three resources work together. God can use His Holy Spirit to counsel husbands through their wives. Many times God has used Katie to warn me, correct me, encourage me, or direct me. There have been times when Katie has shared Scripture with me, or given me her thoughts on a passage and it helped me better understand God's Word.

For any who would question whether a husband should listen to his wife, Scripture gives a powerful example. The context is the Roman prefect Pontius Pilate who was sitting in judgment over the trial and crucifixion of Jesus. During the trial, Pilate's wife sent him a message: "Have nothing to do with that just man, for I have suffered many things today in a dream because of Him" (Matthew 27:19). Pilate rejected her counsel, and we all know the consequences. Could there be a better example in all of history of a time when a husband should have listened to his wife?

I would like to share about a time I believe God really used Katie to direct me, and it is when I was an associate pastor at Grace Baptist Church in Lemoore, California. Although it was a wonderful season of life for me, Katie found it difficult because she thought God had gifted me to shepherd my own church. The senior pastor shared Katie's thoughts, so she had confirmation from him as well.

When we found Woodland Christian Church, Katie wanted me to take the position, but I was struggling. I enjoyed my job at Grace Baptist, I do not like change, and I did not want to say goodbye to so many people I loved. Plus, I had security that would be lost if I took the position at Woodland Christian Church, because there had been conflict, leaving the congregation fairly small. One of the deacons had the integrity to tell me:

"Based on our savings, if the giving remains the same, we will only be able to pay you for eight months."

I paint this picture to explain how hard it was for me to accept the position. Looking back, Katie's encouragement is one of the only reasons I was able to make the move. There is one more detail to the story, but I will save that for later. For now, I simply want to share that it was trusting that God was using Katie that allowed me to become the senior pastor of Woodland Christian Church.

Submission Does Not Mean That Wives Are Inferior

A common criticism of submission sounds something like this: "If wives are supposed to submit to their husbands, then wives are not equal to their husbands. Since God made men and women equal, wives do not have to submit." Do we apply this thinking to the other relationships we discussed that involve submission? Do we think parents are superior to their children, elders are superior to their congregations, governments are superior to the people they govern, or employers are superior to their employees? Not at all. The same logic dictates that a wife's submission to her husband does not in any way imply that husbands are superior to their wives.

Perhaps the best example of this occurs in the relationship between God the Son and God the Father. Consider these verses demonstrating Jesus's submission:

- In John 5:30, Jesus stated: "I do not seek My own will but the will of the Father who sent Me."
- In John 6:38, Jesus said: "I have come down from heaven, not to do My own will, but the will of Him who sent Me."
- In Matthew 26:39, Jesus prayed only a few hours before His crucifixion, "O My Father, if it is possible, let this cup pass from Me; nevertheless, not as I will, but as You will."

Does the Son's submission to the Father indicate that the Son is inferior to the Father? Absolutely not. Jesus made His equality with the Father very evident:

- In John 10:30, Jesus claimed, "I and My Father are one."
- In John 17:20–22, Jesus said, "I [pray] for those who will believe in Me . . . that they all may be one, *as You, Father, are in Me, and I in You* . . . that they may be one *just as We are one.*"

Those who believe submission means women are inferior to men must also assert that the Son is inferior to the Father. If we acknowledge that the Son can be both submissive to the Father and equal with Him, we must also acknowledge that wives can be submissive to their husbands while still being equal with them.

In some ways, the Son's submissiveness to the Father and the unity, equality, and oneness they share is a beautiful picture of a wife's submissiveness to her husband and the unity, equality, and oneness they should share. To make the parallel with marriage even stronger, 1 Corinthians 11:3 states: "the head of woman is man, and the head of Christ is God." Just as the Son sees the Father as His head a wife should see her husband as her head.

Following Jesus's Example of Submission

A wife should then be encouraged to submit to her husband by looking at Jesus's example in submitting to the Father. In Peter's discussion of submission, he also stated: "For to this you were called, because Christ also suffered for us, *leaving us an example, that you should follow His steps*" (1 Peter 2:21). Jesus set down the example for us to follow. This does not apply only to wives' submitting to their husbands but to any relationship previously mentioned. When children demonstrate submission to parents, congregations demonstrate submission to elders, believers demonstrate submission to government, and employees demonstrate submission to employers, they are demonstrating the heart of Christ. A submissive heart is a heart like Christ's. To submit is to be like Christ.

Just as Jesus is the premier example of submission, so Satan offers the premier example of rebellion. Scripture provides vivid images of Satan's original rejection of God as his head, which resulted in his being cast down and out of heaven (Isaiah 14:12–20; Ezekiel 28:12–19). Then, in the Garden of Eden, we see him as a serpent stirring up similar rebellion in Eve. Consider the parallelism between the words he spoke to himself and the words he spoke to Eve:

- Isaiah 14:14—"I will ascend above the heights of the clouds, *I will be like the Most High.*"
- Genesis 3:5b—"Your eyes will be opened, and *you will be like God.*"

Satan is saying here in essence: "You do not need to submit to God. You can have His position instead." To be rebellious and reject the authority God has placed over us—whether parents, church leadership, government, employers, or husbands as head of the family—is to follow Satan's example.

But let's not conclude with our focus on Satan. When we think of submission, we should think about:

- How Jesus was willing to submit—perfectly
- What He was willing to submit to—the wrath of God that our sins deserve
- Why He was willing to submit—His great love for us

Nobody has ever had as much to submit to as Jesus did. Nobody has ever submitted to any trial or suffering as well as Jesus did. Whenever we are facing a situation that calls for submission, we should be encouraged by the example Jesus set for us.

Chapter Fourteen

Putting Your Husband in a Position to Lead

S ome husbands do not lead because they believe their wives are going to fight whatever decision they make. As a result, they do not take their responsibilities seriously. Some wives say they want their husbands to lead, but what they really mean is: "I want my husband to do what I want." Let me conclude my story about accepting the senior pastor position at Woodland Christian Church. I would summarize it like this: Katie put me in a position to lead.

Though Katie encouraged me to take the position, she could see I was hesitant. I remember her clearly saying, "If this move ends up being a mistake and we went there because of me, I couldn't live with that. The only way I can feel good about this decision is if *you* make it. I respect your leadership, and I believe God will direct you. Whatever you decide, I will support you."

I knew how hard it was for Katie to say this because of how much she wanted me to take the position. Her putting the responsibility so squarely on my shoulders made me take the decision even more seriously. In some ways, it was easier when Katie was telling me what she wanted, but the moment she told me I had to decide, I could feel the weight settle on me.

139

When a wife says, "I will support whatever you decide," a husband has no choice but to lead. Some husbands do not feel the weight of responsibility because their wives are too busy trying to take the mantle of leadership upon themselves. Some wives even take charge and then complain, "I am so tired of not being able to count on my husband to make decisions."

In marriage counseling, wives have told me, "I have to do it because if I don't, it won't get done." I often respond, "How do you know? Maybe your husband would do it if he knew you would not. Your husband might be so used to your taking matters into your own hands that the thought of leading does not even cross his mind!" When wives recognize that it is not their God-given role to lead and place the responsibility squarely on their husbands' shoulders, they increase the likelihood their husbands will take their leadership roles seriously.

If a wife really wants her husband to lead, she should put him in the position to do so. Get behind him. Encourage him. Make him feel responsible. Then, when a husband starts to lead, a wife needs to make sure she does not complain about his decisions or criticize him for not doing things the way she wants. She needs to embrace the decision he makes, and resist the temptation to take over. Helen Andelin, founder of the Fascinating Womanhood Movement for promoting biblical marriage writes:

> When a woman hands back the [reins] to her husband, she must let go completely. She must turn her back on it, come what may. If he makes a mess of it, let him suffer the consequences. Refer all [questions] to him. Don't shield him in any way. He must suffer. That is the only way he will learn [to lead]."[20]

To be clear, if a wife steps back to let her husband lead, things might go poorly at first. I do not want to give the impression that following biblical principles means everything works out perfectly. Some things,

---

[20] Helen Andelin, *Secrets of Fascinating Womanhood* (Zealand, 1989), p. 92.

undoubtedly, will fall through the cracks. If a husband has never led before, he probably will not hit the ground running. Though we hope a husband will quickly step up if a wife does not take over, he might not. When a husband is not used to being in the driver's seat, he might be all over the road at first. But the wife needs to decide: "The driver's seat is not mine. It belongs to my husband." Regardless of how well or poorly a husband leads, the responsibility still belongs to him.

If a wife communicates this reality through her actions, she can be confident that at some point he will figure out: "Wow, she expects me to be in charge. She isn't going to take over. I'd better get my act together."

Embracing Your Husband's Leadership Style

A wife should not embrace sin in her husband's life, but she should embrace his personality. This is the man she chose to marry. His personality is not something she has any right to try to change, because that is the way God created him. Since men have different personalities, they will also do things differently. There is nothing wrong with that, because there is not one right or wrong way to lead.

The greatest men in Scripture had different personalities and, as a result, they led differently. King David was a military-minded man. First he was a soldier, then a general, and even as a king he still often led his men into battle. His son, King Solomon, in contrast was another great leader, but there is no record of him fighting even one battle. The prophets were also very different from each other. Elijah was a loner, but his successor, Elisha, was more social. Jeremiah was sensitive and emotional. Isaiah was a family man with a wife and children.

The judges delivered Israel from their oppressors, but each accomplished that goal uniquely:

- Ehud used his left-handedness to conceal a dagger and assassinate the king of Moab.
- Samson used brute strength to defeat his enemies.
- Jephthah was diplomatic, sending messengers to Israel's enemy.

- Each of these men was a successful leader, but each worked differently.
- What if Jephthah's wife said: "Instead of sending those messengers, why don't you try to be like Ehud and assassinate the king of Ammon?"
- What if Ehud's wife said: "Why are you so sneaky? Why don't you be a real man like Samson for a change?"

Even if a wife could change her husband, she would encounter just as many frustrations with her "new" man as she had with the "old" one. For example, imagine a wife has a very consistent, steady husband, but she thinks he is kind of boring. She wishes he was more adventurous. She wishes he had more ideas, and did not take so long to think about things. Then her husband becomes that kind of man. At first it seems great. They jump in the car for a spontaneous trip without bothering to plan out the details. He leaves his job for one that sounds more exciting, which means the family gets to move and experience new surroundings.

But soon the wife finds herself struggling with all the change in their lives. She thinks her husband makes decisions hastily. She wishes their lives were more consistent. Pretty soon she is longing for her old, steady, "boring" husband.

Or the reverse. A wife has a very decisive husband, but she wishes he listened better and did not make up his mind so quickly. Then imagine she gets her gentler, more patient husband. At first it is great because he listens so well. He considers what she and the kids want, but pretty soon she is frustrated because it takes him so long to make up his mind. The kids misbehave, but he is not as quick to discipline them. She even wishes he was firmer with her because she does not like that she can walk all over him. Pretty soon, she starts missing her strong, decisive husband.

The point is every husband's personality has advantages and disadvantages. While a wife might wish her husband were different in certain ways, those differences would come with accompanying frustrations.

This is one reason a wife should not encourage her husband to be like other men. Instead, she should be thankful for the personality God gave him. When God created women as comparable helpers for their husbands, He did not make all wives the same any more than He made all husbands the same. We discussed that women have different strengths to complement their husbands' needs and weaknesses. Similarly, the different leadership style God gives each husband is meant to complement the particular needs of his wife and family.

It Is Not Leadership Style, but a Heart for God That Matters

Repeatedly kings were said to be good if they were like King David:

- 1 Kings 15:11—Asa did what was right in the eyes of the LORD, *as did his father David.*
- 2 Kings 18:3—[Hezekiah] did what was right in the sight of the LORD, *according to all that his father David had done.*
- 2 Kings 22:2a—[Josiah] did what was right in the sight of the LORD, and *walked in all the ways of his father David.*

Or kings were said to be bad if they were like King Jeroboam:

- 1 Kings 16:19a—[Zimri] committed in doing evil in the sight of the LORD, in *walking in the way of Jeroboam.*
- 1 Kings 16:25–26a—Omri did evil in the eyes of the LORD . . . For *he walked in all the ways of Jeroboam.*
- 1 Kings 22:52a—[Ahaziah] did evil in the sight of the LORD, and *walked . . . in the way of Jeroboam.*

When Scripture says a king is like David, does it mean that he was a shepherd or that he slew giants? No, it means that king had a heart for God like David, the "man after [God's] own heart" (1 Samuel 13:14; Acts 13:22).

Jeroboam became king and then he installed golden calves that led Israel away from God (1 Kings 12:25–33). When Scripture says a king is like Jeroboam, does it mean that he built calf idols? No, it means that king was evil like Jeroboam was evil.

Men have never been good or bad leaders because they led a certain way. Men have always been good or bad leaders because they either served God or they did not. That was the case in the Old Testament, and it is the same today.

Regardless of personality or leadership style, every godly man is called to do certain things. He must pray with his family, be a student of the Word, disciple his children, and serve the body of Christ. While there is liberty regarding how men lead their homes, no man has the liberty to say:

- "I don't pray with my family because that's not really my leadership style."
- "I don't take my family to church because that's not really my personality."
- "I don't read the Bible with my family because I'm not really into reading."

If a man is not doing these things, he is failing as a spiritual leader regardless of his leadership style or personality. Every husband should keep two things in mind:

1. No matter how many good things a man does for his family, he cannot be a great husband without being a great spiritual leader. No amount of family vacations, completed projects around the house, or time with the wife and children, can take the place of the greatest call God has on a husband's life.
2. Whatever husbands do in the work place, even what they do in the church, pales in comparison to what they need to be doing in the home. First Timothy 3:5 states: "If a man does not know how to rule his own house, how will he take care of the church of God?" So while it is wonderful to serve our brothers and sisters in Christ, God states that it is even more important for a husband to serve his wife and children by leading them well spiritually.

A Wife Can Make Her Husband's Spiritual Leadership Easier

When Katie and I got together, I really wanted to impress her. I remember one of our first Bible studies as a couple. I decided to show Katie the relationship between three passages of Scripture: one in Isaiah, one in 2 Kings, and one in 2 Chronicles. It was probably the most confusing Bible study ever taught. Let's just say that by the time we finished three hours later, I did not look impressive—just weird. Later that day, however, I overheard Katie on the phone telling a friend: "I am so thankful to have met a man who will read the Bible with me."

You can imagine what an encouragement that was to hear. Sadly, I have met husbands who are reluctant to read the Bible or pray in front of their wives because they are afraid of the wife's reaction if they do not measure up to a pastor or Bible teacher on the radio. Wives, let me give you some encouragements as well as some discouragements to make your husband's spiritual leadership easier.

Be Encouraged To . . .

Thank your husband when he takes the family to church—sadly, this is more than many men do. There are women who would give just about anything to have a husband worshiping the Lord next to them. Ladies, do not take that for granted!

Encourage your husband when he prays or reads Scripture with you—he might fumble every word he says, but you should still applaud him for his spiritual leadership. Recognize that you are among a small percentage of wives whose husbands engage in these disciplines with them. Hold his hand when you pray, and thank the Lord for giving you such a godly man.

Support your husband with the children—help get the kids together for times of worship. When your husband reads the Bible with the family, set an example to your children by being attentive. Encourage the children to express appreciation for a father willing to do what few men do.

Be Discouraged From . . .

Needless debate—this is a tough issue, because I do not want to discourage wives from asking their husbands questions or even disagreeing if they say something wrong. But if your husband believes he is going to face an argument every time you open the Bible together, you are going to have a husband who does not open the Bible with you.

Katie and I were once counseling a couple whom we finally persuaded to read the Bible together. When I asked the husband later how it was going, he told me they had stopped because whenever they read together, his wife constantly challenged him to the point that he never wanted to read the Bible with her again.

Needless comparisons—wives, I implore you to never, under any circumstances, compare your husband negatively with some other man. This is your husband. Be thankful for him. If he does not have the gift of teaching, which is a spiritual gift the Holy Spirit gives to some believers and not to others, then he is probably already nervous about reading or praying in front of you or the kids. Those who do not have the gift of teaching are not inferior or less spiritual but simply have different spiritual gifts. Some of the godliest men I have known would struggle terribly if they had to teach in front of others.

The last thing any husband needs is to hear that he does not sound like the pastor on television. Do not expect a sermon or Billy Graham Crusade when your husband opens the Bible with you. The power is in God's Word and not in your husband's teaching ability. If your husband is reading Scripture, trust that it is washing over the family and doing its work of bringing spiritual cleansing and sanctification as we discussed in Ephesians 5:26.

Let's imagine a hypothetical situation. A husband has been reading this book and feels convicted about being a better spiritual leader. He has not been reading the Bible with his family, but he knows he should.

Understandably, he is nervous about doing so. He does not know how his family is going to respond. He is asking himself questions such as "What if I don't know what to say? What if they ask me a question I can't answer? Where should I start? What if I don't sound like Pastor Bill?"

All day at work he has been summoning up his courage, and he has decided that today is the day. As soon as dinner is over, he is going to ask his family to get their Bibles. Fast-forward a few hours. Dinner is over and the husband's heart is racing, but he still manages to say, "Tonight, we're going to do something different. Why don't we all grab our Bibles and we'll read a passage together?"

Now imagine his wife says:

- "Do we have to do this right now? I wanted to get the table cleaned up."
- "Is that the version of the Bible we're going to use? Can we use this instead?"
- "Is this the passage we're going to read? Why did you pick this one?"
- "Is that how you pronounce his name?"
- "When I was listening to the pastor on the radio, that's not what he said about this verse."
- "I don't think that's right."
- "Can you ask Mike if that's correct?"
- "Wow, this first Bible study sure is long!"

Will this husband ever read the Bible with his family again? Probably not. Now imagine this. Same husband, same conviction, same nervousness all day. Dinner is over. He tells his family to get their Bibles and his wife says:

- "I am so excited!"
- "This is such an answer to prayer."
- "I am very proud of you!"

- "I know not many men do this with their families. I feel very blessed to have you as my husband."

Imagine his wife says to the children:

- "Isn't this great? What a wonderful daddy you have!"
- "Let's go get our Bibles. Don't worry about the dishes. We'll take care of that later." This statement alone will get the kids excited!

They pray when the study is over and his wife says, "Lord, I am so thankful to have such a godly man. Thank You that he will read the Bible with us. We are so blessed. Help him lead our family. What a huge responsibility he has. You have called me to be his helper, so please help me to help him." These sorts of actions from a wife will diffuse a husband's fears and infuse him with the confidence and encouragement he needs.

In conclusion:

- Wife, be your husband's biggest supporter. Encourage him when he prays and reads the Word with his family.
- Husband, do these things that God has called you to do and that will gain your family's respect.

Part VI: 1 Peter 3:1–7

A Wife's Beauty and a Husband's Treatment

Chapter Fifteen

Winning Over Your Husband

1 Peter 3:1–2—Wives, likewise, be submissive to your own
husbands, that even if some do not obey the word, they,
without a word, may be won by the conduct of their wives,
when they observe your chaste conduct accompanied by fear.

In the following chapters, we will take a close look at another key
marriage passage in Scripture: 1 Peter 3:1–7. These verses offer rich
additional illumination to questions we already addressed:

- Are there any benefits to submission?
- What is true beauty?
- How should husbands live with their wives?

The first instruction in this passage is directed to wives and once again
deals with submission—but with a new twist. We have established that
wives are not expected to submit to abuse, sin, or even other men. Yet, is
a spiritually mature wife expected to submit to a spiritually *im*mature
husband? According to the apostle Peter's instruction above, the answer
is clear. A spiritually mature wife is not only expected to submit to a
spiritually immature husband, but also to submit to a spiritually bankrupt
husband or, we could say, an unbeliever.

How do we know that is what Peter had in mind? Each human author
of the Bible had his own style of writing. When Peter mentioned husbands

who do not obey the Word, we know that he was referring to unbelieving husbands because he used similar terminology for non-Christians elsewhere. For example, in 1 Peter 1:2 he described believers as "elect according to the foreknowledge of God the Father, in sanctification of the Spirit, *for obedience*." Peter equated obedience with salvation, and rightly so. Believers should be obedient. In 1 Peter 2:8, he similarly described unbelievers as "*being disobedient* to the word." Since he used obedience to refer to a believer and disobedience to refer to an unbeliever, Peter's description of men who "do not obey the word" in 1 Peter 3:1 means he was referring to unbelieving husbands. This does not mean the man is a scoundrel. He may be kind, affectionate, and hold to a high moral standard; however, if he has not taken the first step of obedience—that is, the obedience of faith—then he is properly identified as disobedient.

This should be an encouragement to wives whose Christian husbands are not as spiritually mature as they would like. Although submitting to an immature believing husband may be difficult at times, it is not as difficult as submitting to an unbelieving husband. Since God's Word commands wives to submit to unsaved husbands (within the parameters discussed in Chapter 13), how much more should wives be willing to submit to spiritually immature believing husbands? A Christian husband might not be as spiritually mature as his wife longs for, but at least she can be thankful that he is a Christian.

What If You Are Married to an Unbeliever?

For wives who find themselves in marriages with unbelieving husbands, Peter offers encouragement and hope. Through a wife's example of godly submission, her husband may be won to faith in Jesus. In a parallel passage found in 1 Corinthians 7:13–16, Paul explains why a believing wife is called to submit to her unbelieving spouse rather than simply leave him to find a marriage partner more compatible with her spiritual commitment:

> And a woman who has a husband who does not believe, if he is willing to live with her, let her not divorce him. For the unbelieving husband is sanctified by the wife, and the unbelieving

wife is sanctified by the husband; otherwise your children would be unclean, but now they are holy. But if the unbeliever departs, let him depart; a brother or a sister is not under bondage in such cases. But God has called us to peace. For how do you know, O wife, whether you will save your husband? Or how do you know, O husband, whether you will save your wife?

Paul's teaching is two-fold. First, believing spouses are called to remain in the marriage relationship insofar as it is up to them. "Sanctified" means "set apart" or "holy." By staying married, the believing spouse is able to have a spiritual influence on the unbelieving spouse. The unbelieving spouse is being "set apart" to constant exposure of the believing spouse's faith. This can allow the unbelieving spouse to come to faith as well. Logically, we understand that one of the best ways for unbelievers to come to salvation is through relationships with believers. An unbeliever could have no more intimate relationship with a believer than through marriage.

Likewise, the children of the marriage are far more likely to be exposed to godly living through the believing spouse remaining in the home and creating a Christian environment. The alternative breaks up the home, possibly leaving the children in the primary custody of the unbelieving parent. In 1 Corinthians 7:13–16, this issue is directed primarily at the believing wife, perhaps because in the time period in which Paul was writing, husbands had sole legal possession of their children. A believing wife who abandoned the marriage would also be abandoning her children to the custody and sole influence of an unbelieving husband. As Paul concluded, a believer staying in the marriage may provide just the influence necessary to bring an unbelieving spouse or child to faith. It is not guaranteed, however. Paul wrote, "How do you know . . .?" pointing out that it is only a possibility—not a certainty.

The second matter Paul addressed was an unbelieving spouse who chooses to leave the believing spouse. While believers are instructed to stay in the marriage and be an influence to win the spouse to faith, Paul also makes clear that they cannot force an unbelieving spouse to remain. This is especially pertinent when a wife or husband comes to Christ after marriage, a life-changing circumstance an unbelieving spouse may not accept.

Notice that Paul's advice is based on "God [calling] us to peace." This is to say that if the conversion of one spouse to Christianity has become the focal point of continued conflict, then the believing spouse should not engage in conflict over the unbelieving spouse's departure. This would be antithetical to the Christian's calling to peace. Additionally, unbelievers are never won to Christ through heated conflict. Paul was asserting that it is more important to be true to the Christian testimony of peace than to attempt to keep an unbeliever in a marriage by force or argumentation. This does elevate the Christian faith above even an unstable marriage. It is better to let the unbeliever depart than to sully Christ's reputation.

Let me be clear, however, that Paul's permission for Christians to allow an unbelieving spouse to "depart" should not be interpreted as permission to divorce. As we have already discussed in connection with abuse, a separated spouse is commanded to remain single while seeking reconciliation: "If [a wife] does depart, let her remain unmarried or be reconciled to her husband. And a husband is not to divorce his wife. A wife is bound to her husband as long as he lives" (1 Corinthians 7:11, 39; Romans 7:2). The principle is that even when separated from an unbelieving or sinful spouse, a believer may still be an influence for change and repentance through faithfulness to the unsaved person. This is why God's design is always reconciliation and never divorce.

I will be the first to acknowledge that marriage can be difficult enough for two believers—and much more so for a believer married to an unbeliever. But how tragic it is—and disobedient to God's Word—for Christians to divorce an unbelieving spouse when that believer constitutes the unbeliever's greatest chance to be drawn to faith. I have heard Christians talk about wanting to leave an unbelieving husband or wife, usually adding how terrible the person is. I do not doubt what they say, but in my mind I am thinking: "Yes, this sounds terrible, but the worse you make the person sound, the more obvious it is just how much your spouse needs Christ. And that person needs to be exposed to Christ through you!"

A Wife's Nagging and a Husband's Stubbornness

Note two contrasting points from 1 Peter 3:1. Peter tells wives:

- How *not to* try to win their husbands—with words.
- How *to* try to win their husbands—with their conduct.

In Genesis 3:16, God told Eve, "Your desire shall be for your husband, and he shall rule over you." This verse reveals two struggles husbands and wives will have as a result of the fall. We already discussed that the first half of the verse looks to wives trying to control their husbands. This often manifests itself as nagging, as shown by a number of verses in Proverbs. Here are a few:

- Proverbs 19:13b—The contentions of a wife are a continual dripping.
- Proverbs 21:9 and 25:24—Better to dwell in a corner of a housetop, than in a house shared with a contentious woman.
- Proverbs 21:19—Better to dwell in the wilderness, than with a contentious and angry woman.

The second half of the verse, "And he shall rule over you" subtly reveals the corresponding struggle men have with stubbornness. God created men to be leaders, so by nature they are less receptive to having their wives tell them what to do.

Two truths make the tension between husbands and wives even worse:

1. Husbands seem to struggle with stubbornness even more when they feel they are being nagged.
2. Wives seem to struggle with nagging even more when they feel their husbands are being stubborn.

This can create a vicious cycle that sucks the joy out of marriage. God is aware of this, so He has revealed how to bring it to an end—not with words, but with godly behavior.

If you are a believing wife, I know there are things you want your husband to do, such as read the Bible with you and pray with you. Perhaps you also want your husband to do things of a less spiritual nature, such as finish a project around the house or take the family on a trip he promised some time ago. There might also be certain things that you want your husband to stop doing, such as watching ungodly things or spending too much time on a certain activity.

The truth is, nagging your husband will not bring him any closer to being the man you desire him to be or increase the likelihood of his doing what you want. On the contrary, since men are stubborn, nagging will probably make him less inclined to do what you want and could possibly even push him in the opposite direction. What a wife needs to do instead is obey Peter's command to win over her husband, not with words, but with godly conduct.

Here is a practical example of this. Earlier, I shared about my addiction to World of Warcraft when Katie and I were first married. One reason I felt so convicted about my behavior was that I had married a wonderful woman, and even at the worst of my addiction, Katie continued being a godly wife. If she had nagged me or mistreated me in some way, I would not have felt as bad.

Now do not get me wrong. Katie let me know how much it bothered her that I was playing. I have already mentioned that she had a little breakdown over it, but she spoke to me honestly out of her pain, instead of in anger. Had she yelled at me, I would have felt more justified in playing because I would have thought that she did not deserve better. It was Katie's godly conduct while I was being a lame husband that helped convict me of my selfishness.

To provide some balance here, I am not advising wives to refrain from ever asking their husbands to do certain things, or not do certain things, or from giving their husbands reminders. We have already discussed that

God created a wife to be a "helper" to her husband. Sometimes husbands forget things, and a reminder (or two) can be a real blessing.

Another struggle common to men could be summed up with the word "oblivious." Sometimes husbands walk around having little idea how much they have hurt their wives, children, or friends. They are unaware of how their wives, or anyone else for that matter, feel about what they are doing or not doing. Husbands need their wives to point certain things out to them.

Wives should share with their husbands what they want and how they feel, but they should keep two points in mind:

1. The frequency with which a wife says these things is important. At some point, a request made a few times moves from being reasonable to nagging.

2. The way a wife makes her requests is important. Yelling and disrespecting a husband will not convict him. Lovingly and respectfully petitioning him about the way he is acting and the pain he is causing will. When a wife speaks to her husband in this way, he will likely feel terrible for mistreating such a wonderful woman.

Husbands in turn need to let their wives know when they have moved from being helpful to nagging, but in a gentle and loving way. Husbands who respond cruelly to their wives are not going to help their wives stop nagging. When a husband raises his voice at his wife he is sinning, but he is also pushing her to move from nagging to yelling in response.

A Warning about Winning

A wife can win over her husband, but not necessarily in a positive way. We have already discussed two examples of this:

- Sarah convinced Abraham to take Hagar as a concubine.
- Jezebel convinced Ahab to steal Naboth's vineyard.

Scripture gives another example of a man who made a habit of allowing the women in his life to win him over with their words, and it resulted in disastrous consequences. Ironically Samson was the strongest man in history, but he was overcome by the persistence of two women who could be termed the Queens of Nagging.

Samson chose a Philistine for a wife. During the wedding festivities, he posed a riddle to thirty men from his bride's town. If they did not solve the riddle, each of them would have to supply him with a set of clothing. If they solved it, he would supply each of them with a set. Wanting the answer, the men went to Samson's wife, who agreed to help her fellow Philistines obtain the answer from her husband. For seven days she wept and complained: "You only hate me! You do not love me! You have posed a riddle to the sons of my people, but you have not explained it to me" (Judges 14:16).

Samson's new bride "pressed him so much" (Judges 14:17) that he finally told her the answer, and she told the Philistine men. Feeling betrayed, Samson rejected his wife and she married one of the thirty men (Judges 14:20).

Sadly, Samson did not learn from his mistake. Sometime later he fell in love with another Philistine woman named Delilah (Judges 16:4). By this time the Philistines were furious over Samson's successful attacks against them. They offered Delilah a large reward if she would find out the source of his great strength so they could defeat him.

Delilah nagged Samson and he told her lies on three separate occasions (Judges 16:6–14). Each time she would wait until Samson was asleep, then she would call the Philistines and act on the lie he had told her. Since Samson was lying, he was able to easily defeat the Philistines. Finally, Delilah played the victim: "How can you say, 'I love you,' when your heart is not with me? You have mocked me these three times, and have not told me where your great strength lies" (Judges 16:15).

Does this sound familiar? It is almost identical to Samson's first wife. Delilah "pestered him daily with her words and pressed him so that his soul was vexed to death" (Judges 16:16). She made him so miserable with her nagging that he wished he were dead. In Judges 16:17 he finally admitted:

"No razor has ever come upon my head, for I have been a Nazirite to God from my mother's womb. If I am shaven, then my strength will leave me, and I shall become weak, and be like any other man."

Samson knew that Delilah would turn him over to the Philistines, but he told her anyway and it is a strong testament to the power of a woman's nagging. In a scene that is painful even to read, Delilah cut off Samson's hair while he slept and his strength was gone. The Philistines captured him, put his eyes out, and turned him into a slave. He remained in captivity until his last-ditch stand that resulted in his death along with three thousand Philistines.

The lesson is some wives manipulate their husbands like the two women in Samson's life. They play the victim and act as though they are being mistreated. They nag until their husbands' souls, like Samson's, are vexed to the point where death feels a better alternative. The wife's words finally wear down the husband until he gives in.

Winning by Godly Conduct

Wives will not win over their unbelieving husbands by what they say, but they might win them over by their lifestyle. The gracious submission of a Christian woman to her unsaved husband is the strongest evangelistic tool she has. Just what does this look like in practical terms? Comparing 1 Peter 2:18 with 1 Peter 3:1–2 can help with the answer because of the parallel language between the verses:

- "Servants, be submissive to your masters" is similar to "Wives . . . be submissive to your own husbands."
- "Not only to the good and gentle, but also to the harsh" is similar to "even if some do not obey the word."
- "With all fear" is similar to "your chaste conduct accompanied by fear."

In both verses, it is important to understand that this is not speaking of servants or wives submitting out of fear of their masters or husbands, but submitting out of fear of God. The NIV says, "Slaves, *in reverent fear of God* submit yourselves to your masters." First Peter 1:17 supports that this is the intent in both passages because Peter used similar terminology earlier in speaking to believers as a whole: "If you call on the Father . . . conduct yourselves throughout the time of your stay here *in fear.*"

Servants submit to their masters, and wives submit to their husbands, not out of fear of a man but out of respect and reverence for God. When an unbelieving husband sees this heart for God it will be a powerful witness. His wife's godly behavior will convict him to be a godlier husband. Her life will speak louder to him than any words.

If a wife wants her husband to read God's Word more, pray more, or be a godlier man, rather than nagging him, she herself should read God's Word more, pray more, and be a godlier woman. Wives should be encouraged by Jesus's promise to send the Holy Spirit in John 16:8: "When [the Holy Spirit] has come, *He will convict the world of sin.*" Notice the emphasis is on the Holy Spirit doing the convicting. This includes husbands, unbelieving or otherwise! Wives are not supposed to take over the Holy Spirit's role in their husbands' lives. Wives should pray, and then trust the Holy Spirit to do the work Jesus promised He would do.

No husband can sit at home being unspiritual and lame while watching his spiritual wife without feeling ashamed. A husband might pretend that he is not convicted, and his wife might not be able to tell by looking at him that he feels convicted, but he does. In contrast, when a wife is unsubmissive, angry, and nagging, the husband does not see God through her and as a result avoids feeling convicted at all.

Jesus Sets the Example of Godly Conduct Versus Words

The greatest example, not just for wives, but for all of us, is Jesus Himself. In the apostle Peter's discussion of submission, he emphasized the way Jesus demonstrated godly conduct through actions and not words:

For to this you were called, because Christ also suffered for us, leaving us an example, that you should follow His steps . . . who, when He was reviled, did not revile in return; when He suffered, He did not threaten, but committed Himself to Him who judges righteously (1 Peter 2:21–23).

The specific example Peter was referring to was Jesus's conduct during His trials leading up to the crucifixion. He was silent before His accusers, answering them not a word (Isaiah 53:7; Matthew 27:12; Acts 8:32). He was willing to endure the shame and eventually the cross itself for our sakes. While we were yet unbelieving and lost in our sins, Jesus was willing to lay down His life to win our salvation. This is the example to which we are called, whether wives or husbands, in being willing to live in such a way that unbelieving spouses may be won to salvation through the conduct of a believing spouse.

Chapter Sixteen

A Woman's Greater Beauty

*1 Peter 3:3–4—Do not let your adornment be merely
outward—arranging the hair, wearing gold, or putting on fine
apparel—rather let it be the hidden person of the heart, with
the incorruptible beauty of a gentle and quiet spirit, which is
very precious in the sight of God.*

In 1 Peter 3:1–2, the apostle made the point that a wife's greatest asset in winning over her husband is godly character. Then in the following verses he lays out exactly what such a godly woman looks like. He begins with her physical appearance because this is a good indicator of her spiritual appearance. It would not be too much to say that what comes forth on the outside was produced from the inside.

The Greek word for "adornment" in 1 Peter 3:3 is *kosmos*, related to the English word "cosmetic." *Kosmos* is an umbrella term that encompasses everything related to the physical appearance—clothing, makeup, or jewelry. Note that Peter's instruction does not forbid outward adornment: "Do not let your adornment be *merely* outward." The use of the word "merely" means a woman's beauty should not come only from outward appearances. The NASB and Amplified Bible render this: "your adornment must not be merely external." Women are not being instructed to neglect their appearance; instead they are being told that outward beauty should not be their primary focus. For any readers who have been made to feel guilty about any form of external beautification, let me point out that Scripture actually makes positive references to jewelry and fine clothing.

Proverbs 25:12 states, "Like an earring of gold and an ornament of fine gold is a wise rebuker to an obedient ear." Gold jewelry is compared to the way an obedient ear accepts instruction. If outward adornments such as earrings were immoral, Scripture would hardly compare them to wise behavior. Likewise, the beautiful bride in Song of Solomon is complimented on her jewelry: "Your cheeks are lovely with ornaments, your neck with chains of gold. We will make you ornaments of gold with studs of silver" (Song of Solomon 1:10–11).

We discussed the Virtuous Wife of Proverbs 31, and it is significant that she was not applauded for outward simplicity or plainness. Instead, she was applauded for the way she adorned her family and herself: "All her household is clothed with scarlet. She makes tapestry for herself; her clothing is fine linen and purple" (Proverbs 31:21b–22). In that time period, scarlet, fine linen, and purple were costly materials worn by the wealthy.

Isaiah 61:10 is a beautiful verse that compares salvation and righteousness with fine clothing, ornaments, and jewelry:

> I will greatly rejoice in the LORD; my soul shall be joyful in my God; for He has clothed me with the garments of salvation, He has covered me with the robe of righteousness, as a bridegroom decks himself with ornaments, and as a bride adorns herself with her jewels.

If outward adornment were immoral, God would hardly compare it with salvation and righteousness.

An even stronger positive reference comes from God's proclamation in Ezekiel 16:11–13 in which He describes His chosen people, Israel, as a beautifully dressed bride:

I adorned you with ornaments, put bracelets on your wrists, and a chain on your neck. And I put a jewel in your nose, earrings in your ears, and a beautiful crown on your head. Thus you were adorned with gold and silver, and your clothing was of fine linen, silk, and embroidered cloth.

If outward adornment were ungodly, we can be sure that God would not outwardly adorn His people as a gift.

Having said this, however, a balance needs to be struck and it is provided for us in 1 Timothy 2:9 where the apostle Paul gives parallel instruction to 1 Peter 3:3: "Women [should] adorn themselves in *modest apparel, with propriety and moderation*, not with braided hair or gold or pearls or costly clothing." Again, the emphasis is not on forbidding women from adorning themselves. Rather, they are told to adorn themselves in a modest and non-extravagant way. The Bible speaks positively of outward adornment, but it also commands moderation and decency. Women must exhibit self-control in their outward beautification.

Outward Appearance Is a Reflection of the Heart

Women should give attention to their outward appearance because each of us—male or female, young or old—is an ambassador of Christ. Women should examine what they wear and why they wear it. Is the motivation to attract attention, or to be a good representative of the Lord?

When a woman dresses immodestly she makes herself into a walking temptation who shows no regard for her brothers in Christ. A woman might dress immodestly because she is insecure, desperate for attention, or does not respect herself. Regardless of the reason, although immodesty manifests itself physically, it begins in the heart. The way a woman looks outwardly says a lot about the way she looks inwardly.

A married woman should keep in mind that the more modestly she dresses, the more attractive she will be to her husband because more is reserved for him alone. Conversely, the more immodestly a wife dresses, the more she makes available to other men, and less is reserved for her husband.

Immodesty is not the only mistake women make when it comes to their appearance. Three others that should be avoided are:

1. Focusing too much on outward appearance, which reveals an unhealthy preoccupation or, worse, an obsession
2. Looking disheveled, tacky, or sloppy, which projects laziness and an unwillingness to invest the effort to look decent
3. Wearing excessive jewelry, makeup, or extravagant clothing, which can be as distracting as having no concern whatsoever for outward appearance

Greater Beauty Is Found Inwardly

In 1 Peter 3, there is a strong relationship between verses 3 and 4. Verse 3 described the natural tendency to be overly focused on outward appearance: "Do not let your adornment be merely outward—arranging the hair, wearing gold, or putting on fine apparel." So in verse 4, Peter encouraged readers to be more focused on the inward: "rather let [your adornment] be the hidden person of the heart, with the incorruptible beauty of a gentle and quiet spirit, which is very precious in the sight of God."

Women should give attention to their outward appearance, but they should give even more attention to their inward appearance. God is more concerned with the way a woman's heart looks than with her face, hair, makeup, or clothing.

The phrase, "hidden person," inspires women to have an inner or unseen beauty that requires looking and searching to find. To see and appreciate this beauty requires an amount of time and energy. Contrast this with the encouragement of secular society. Women are told to "put it all out there" and to be concerned chiefly with outward beauty at the expense of inward beauty. Supposedly you can tell if a woman is beautiful the moment you look at her without making any investment in getting to know her. This turns women into superficial creatures with no dimensions of personality or inner worth.

Inward Beauty Is Incorruptible

In 1997, 2.1 million cosmetic surgeries were performed in the United States; in 2011, 9.2 million were performed.[21] In a fifteen-year-period, the number more than quadrupled. One particularly excessive example took place with a celebrity named Heidi Montag. After ten plastic surgeries in one day, she complained about the scars they left behind:

> Parts of my body definitely look worse than they did pre-surgery.
> This is not what I signed up for! . . . I wish I could jump into a
> time machine and take it all back. Instead, I'm always going to feel
> like Edward Scissorhands.[22]

Even ten plastic surgeries did not give Ms. Montag the beauty she wanted, to say nothing about obtaining beauty that would last the rest of her life. CNN reported:

> What recession? Despite record unemployment, rising health care
> costs and sinking home values, Americans shelled out more than
> $10 billion on cosmetic surgeries and other procedures in 2010 . . .
> Almost half of Americans have less than $10,000 saved for
> retirement, but millions are running off to the plastic surgeon . . .
> What does it mean that despite the worst recession since the

---

[21] The American Society for Aesthetic Plastic Surgery. "Celebrating 15 Years of Trustworthy Plastic Surgery Statistics." Press Center. March 20, 2012. Accessed March 7, 2016. http://www.surgery.org/media/news-releases/celebrating-15-years-of-trustworthy-plastic-surgery-statistics.

[22] Greg Wilson. "Heidi Montag: Plastic Surgery Made Me 'Edward Scissorhands.'" NBC LA. December 21, 2010. Accessed March 7, 2016. http://www.nbclosangeles.com/entertainment/celebrity/Heidi-Montag-Plastic-Surgery-Made-Me-Edward-Scissorhands-112241089.html.

Great Depression, Americans spent more than $10 billion on cosmetic procedures last year?[23]

What it means is that plenty of women—and men too—really want a beauty that does not change with time. The problem is that true incorruptible beauty cannot be found outwardly. Inward beauty is the only beauty that never fades. Since inward beauty does not come from physical appearance, it does not diminish with time or aging. Proverbs 31:30 expresses it this way: "Charm is deceitful and beauty is passing, but a woman who fears the LORD, she shall be praised."

Popular Christian writer J. R. Miller sums up:

> Nowhere but in Christ—can [a wife] find the wisdom and strength she needs, to meet the solemn responsibilities of wifehood. Only in Christ can she find that rich beauty of soul, that gemming of the character, which shall make her lovely in her husband's sight, when the bloom of youth is gone, when the brilliance has faded out of her eyes, and the roses have fled from her cheeks. Only Christ can teach her how to live so as to be blessed, and be a blessing in her married life![24]

Inward beauty does not need any makeup, jewelry, or accessories to be beautiful. Conversely, when a woman does not have inward beauty, no amount of makeup, jewelry, or outward adornment can make her beautiful. A woman who is loud, controlling, and obnoxious might look attractive at first, but the attractiveness will disappear quickly when the lack of inward beauty is revealed. Proverbs 11:22 says: "Like a gold ring in a pig's snout is a beautiful woman without discretion" (ESV). Just as a gold ring cannot make a pig beautiful, physical beauty cannot make an inwardly ugly woman beautiful.

---

[23] Jack Cafferty. "$10 billion spent on cosmetic procedures despite recession" Cafferty File. March 10, 2010. Accessed March 7, 2016. http://caffertyfile.blogs.cnn.com/2010/03/10/10-billion-spent-on-cosmetic-procedures-despite-recession/.

[24] J.R. Miller, *The Home Beautiful*, (Zondervan, 1912), p. 57.

Simply consider any book or movie with a male character falling in love with a woman. The woman is typically presented as laughing, pleasant, and good-tempered as opposed to angrily throwing a tantrum, acting unkindly, or behaving selfishly. Why is that? Even the secular world recognizes inward beauty makes women outwardly attractive, while inward ugliness makes women outwardly unattractive.

There is a ceiling on a woman's outward appearance. She might take care of herself physically, dress nicely, and adorn herself well, but she will still be limited by her genetic material. In contrast, every woman has the potential to develop inward beauty. The obvious question is, "What produces this inward beauty?" It comes from the next quality described in 1 Peter 3:4.

"Spirit" Not "Mouth"

The phrase "gentle and quiet spirit" can be troubling to women who have more extroverted or talkative personalities, or who are gifted to lead and teach. But the phrase is not "gentle and quiet mouth." Peter is not suggesting that women not speak at all. Consider the description of the Virtuous Wife in Proverbs 31:26: "She opens her mouth with wisdom, and on her tongue is the law of kindness." She is applauded for speaking! Since God created women with varying personalities and gifts, His instruction cannot be in conflict with His own creation. Women, regardless of personality or gifting, can still have gentle and quiet spirits.

If Peter is not discouraging women from speaking, what is he saying? He is discouraging women from speaking *a certain way*. The Greek word for "gentle" is *prays*, which means "mildness of disposition, gentleness of spirit, meekness." The word only occurs two other places in Scripture:

1. Matthew 5:5—"Blessed are the meek (*prays*) for they shall inherit the earth."
2. Matthew 21:5—"Behold, your King is coming to you, lowly (*prays*), and sitting on a donkey, a colt, the foal of a donkey."

Prays is used to describe those who will inherit the earth, the Messiah's own disposition, and a godly woman's true beauty.

The Greek word for "quiet" is *hesychios*, which means "tranquil and peaceful." The only other place it occurs is 1 Timothy 2:2 where believers are encouraged to "lead a quiet and peaceable (*hesychios*) life." Taken together, the words "gentle and quiet spirit" describe the way a woman should handle herself and respond to situations in life. She is calm and in control. She is not easily wrought or stirred up.

How does a woman develop this type of spirit? Peter provides the answer in the following verse: "For in this manner, in former times, *the holy women who trusted in God* also adorned themselves" (1 Peter 3:5). A woman develops a gentle and quiet spirit by trusting in the Lord. Holy women of the past who demonstrated gentle and quiet spirits did so through their relationships with God. If a woman trusts God, her spirit will be peaceful and at rest. If a woman does not trust God, she will be filled with anxiety and worry.

God's View of Inward Beauty

One other reason women should be motivated to pursue inward beauty is 1 Peter 3:4, which says it "is very precious in the sight of God." The word for "precious" is *polyteles*, which means "very costly, excellent, of surpassing value." The word occurs only two other times in Scripture:

1. Mark 14:3b—As [Jesus] sat at the table, a woman came having an alabaster flask of very costly (*polyteles*) oil of spikenard. Then she broke the flask and poured it on His head.
2. 1 Timothy 2:9b—Women adorn themselves in modest apparel, with propriety and moderation, not with braided hair or gold or pearls or costly (*polyteles*) clothing.

The parallel between 1 Timothy 2:9 and 1 Peter 3:4 is significant because the same word is used, but in 1 Timothy 2:9 it refers to outward adornment, while in 1 Peter 3:4 it refers to inward beauty. It is as though God is saying: "Women should not pursue outward, fading, expensive beauty, because it is your inward beauty that is truly precious and valuable in My sight." Women should keep two truths in mind:

1. They can be beautiful in society's eyes and ugly in God's eyes.
2. They can be plain or even unattractive in society's eyes and very beautiful in God's eyes.

First Samuel 16:7 confirms: "For the LORD does not see as man sees; for man looks at the outward appearance, but the LORD looks at the heart."

Jesus Was Not Beautiful to the World

A wonderful way to conclude discussing true beauty is by considering what Scripture says about our Savior's looks: "He has no form or comeliness; and when we see Him, there is no beauty that we should desire Him" (Isaiah 53:2). Jesus was humble looking. The word for "comeliness" is *hadar,* and it means "splendor, majesty, honor or glory." Jesus veiled His beauty and glory when He became a man. While few people would try to be unattractive, modern society has made physical beauty something to worship. We should keep in mind that Jesus was able to succeed in pleasing the Father completely without it.

Personally, I do not like pictures of Jesus. They typically make Him very good looking and Caucasian. These pictures do not represent what a first-century Jewish man looked like, but they also put too much emphasis on physical attractiveness. While we cannot say for sure that Jesus was unattractive, Isaiah 53:2 makes clear there was nothing outstanding about His outward appearance that would draw people to Him. Jesus wanted people attracted to Him for other reasons—His humility, love, compassion, and most importantly, the sacrifice He would make for them.

When we think of a gentle and quiet spirit, how can we not think of Christ Himself? Isaiah 53:7 goes on to describe:

He was oppressed and He was afflicted, yet *He opened not His mouth*; He was led as a lamb to the slaughter, and as a sheep before its shearers *is silent,* so *He opened not His mouth.*

Christ's gentle and quiet Spirit is what compelled Him to go to the cross. He truly depicted the greatest manifestation of inward beauty when He submitted to His Father's will.

The Bible's "Perfect" Wife

1 Peter 3:6—As Sarah obeyed Abraham, calling him lord,
whose daughters you are if you do good and are not afraid
with any terror.

The apostle Peter finishes his instruction to women by providing an example of a wife who demonstrated the inner beauty he described in the previous two verses—Abraham's wife, Sarah. That Sarah was chosen as an example for wives should serve as an encouragement to women for two reasons.

First, wives should be encouraged by who Sarah submitted to— Abraham. It might be tempting for women to say: "I wouldn't have any trouble submitting to my husband if he was like Abraham!" While Abraham was one of the greatest men of faith in Scripture, the truth is that being his wife would have been undoubtedly very difficult. God had a unique calling on Abraham's life that involved leaving a comfortable city life in Ur to become a wandering nomad (Genesis 12:1–5; Hebrews 11:8– 10). How many places did they live? How many times did they have to move?

Additionally, Abraham made some foolish decisions. Twice he told Sarah to say she was his sister instead of his wife because he was afraid someone coveting her beauty might murder him in order to seize her for himself:

> [Abraham] said to Sarai his wife, "Indeed I know that you are a woman of beautiful countenance. Therefore it will happen, when the Egyptians see you, that they will say, 'This is his wife'; and *they will kill me*, but they will let you live. *Please say you are my sister, that it may be well with me* for your sake, *and that I may live* because of you" (Genesis 12:11b–13; see also Genesis 20:2).

As a result, Sarah ended up in a pagan king's harem twice, which must have caused Sarah a significant amount of terror. Worse yet, Abraham did not do anything to save her. When his nephew Lot was captured, however, Abraham organized a war party to rescue him. Genesis 14:14–16 records:

> When Abram heard that [Lot] was taken captive, he armed his three hundred and eighteen trained servants . . . and his servants attacked them . . . and also brought back his brother Lot and his goods, as well as the women and the people.

How would that make a wife feel? Far from a strong, brave husband to whom it would be easy to submit and follow, at times Abraham looked like a cowardly, compromising husband willing to endanger his wife to protect himself.

A second reason women should be encouraged by Sarah's being chosen as an example for wives is that she was not always the picture of submission and faith. If Sarah was the perfect wife, it could be pretty discouraging for wives to think they need to emulate her, but in fact Sarah had her own struggles. We have already discussed that she failed when she convinced Abraham to fulfill God's promise of a son and heir through Hagar. She sought to control her husband and it ended up being a disaster on a number of levels. Sarah also failed when God visited Abraham to tell him Sarah would have a child the following year at age 90. Sarah laughed because of her lack of faith and then lied when God confronted her (Genesis 18:12–15).

We could almost wonder why Sarah was chosen as an example of a godly wife at all, but the answer is clearly given in verse 6. Despite Sarah's mistakes, for the most part she was a woman who respected her husband and submitted to him. The verse says Sarah called Abraham "lord," which was a title used often in the Old Testament to show respect. The closest comparable English expression would be addressing a man as "sir." Today's wives may not address their husbands as "lord," but the principle still applies for wives to respect and submit to their husbands as Sarah demonstrated with Abraham.

Wives Submit When They Are Afraid Because They Trust God

The final half of 1 Peter 3:6 offers wives a very special title. They can be identified as "[Sarah's] daughters" if they are "submissive to their own husbands" and "not afraid with any terror." The wording captures how wives may feel at times when it comes to submitting—*terror*. The Greek word for "terror" is *ptoesis*:

- In Luke 21:9 Jesus used the verb form when He told His disciples, "When you hear of wars and commotions, do not be terrified (*ptoeo*)."
- In Luke 24:37 the adjective form is used when Jesus appeared to the disciples after His resurrection and "they were terrified (*ptoeo*) and frightened, and supposed they had seen a spirit."

Terror is stronger than ordinary worries, anxieties, or even fears. Terror is what people feel on a plane about to crash, or when the doctor announces they have cancer, or when they receive a call that one of their children has been in an accident. Apparently, terror is also what wives might feel submitting to their husbands! A wife today probably will not experience the same terror that Sarah experienced in the king's harem when she submitted to Abraham, but there are still plenty of legitimate terrors a woman can face submitting to her husband:

- "What happens if this decision ruins our family?"
- "What happens if he is unable to pay these bills?"
- "What happens if we are not able to eat?"
- "What happens if he shouldn't take this job?"
- "What happens if we move and it ends up being a disaster?"

Let's consider how Sarah handled the terror she felt. This will reveal why she was chosen as the example for wives, and it will allow women to learn how they can receive the honor of being called "[Sarah's] daughters." Based on 1 Peter 3:5 we know that Sarah responded to any terror by "[trusting] in God." This is how she was able to submit to Abraham's poor decisions. She continued to believe that God was in control.

Reading both accounts should be a great encouragement for women because they reveal Sarah's trust was well placed. God kept her captors from consummating a relationship with her:

- Genesis 12:17—But the LORD plagued Pharaoh and his house with great plagues because of Sarai, Abram's wife.
- Genesis 20:3—But God came to Abimelech in a dream by night, and said to him, "Indeed you are a dead man because of the woman whom you have taken, for she is a man's wife."

In both instances, Sarah was rescued from captivity and her deliverance came from God's direct intervention. In the end, Sarah's submission produced blessing not just for her but for her husband as well:

> Then Abimelech took sheep and oxen, and male servants and female servants, and gave them to Abraham, and returned Sarah his wife to him. And Abimelech said, "Behold, my land is before you; dwell where it pleases you." To Sarah he said, "Behold, I have given [Abraham] a thousand pieces of silver. It is a sign of your innocence in the eyes of all who are with you, and before everyone you are vindicated" (Genesis 20:14-16 ESV).

Wives should keep Sarah's example in mind. She experienced some difficult circumstances because of her submission to Abraham, but God protected her, vindicated her, and blessed her and her husband as a result.

In the same way, when a wife is afraid her husband is making the wrong decision, she needs to put her "[trust] in God" and recognize that He is in control. While her husband might not deliver her, God is in charge of the situation. He knows what is best, and He can work through the wife's submission to bring about the best end.

In marriage counseling I often hear women say, "It would be easier for me to submit to my husband if I could trust him" or "I do trust God. I just don't trust my husband." As we see in this passage from 1 Peter, however, a wife's submission is not about trusting her husband but about trusting God. A woman's trust in God combats the fear—or terror—she feels in submitting to her husband. A wife is not expected to submit to her husband because she completely trusts him. A wife is expected to submit to her husband because she completely trusts God. When a wife submits to her husband she is showing her trust in God. Conversely, when a wife does not submit to her husband she is showing she does not trust God.

Why is this the case? God is the One who commands wives to submit to their husbands. When wives obey God in this way they are showing that they trust the God who gave them this command.

Husbands Are Going to Make the Wrong Decisions

Wives might be tempted to say, "If I am supposed to submit to my husband because I trust God, this must mean God will make sure my husband always makes the right decision!" The inevitable reality is that husbands will sometimes make the wrong decisions. Sarah is a good example. She submitted to Abraham and he made the wrong decision—on more than one occasion. Obviously, the fear (or terror) wives can experience when submitting to their husbands comes from the possibility of husbands making the wrong decision. The truth wives need to keep in mind is God will work through a wife's submission, but that does not mean a husband will never make a mistake.

Understandably when a husband is wrong a wife may be tempted to think: "I knew it was going to turn out this way. I should have kept arguing with him. I never should have submitted to him in the first place, and I am never going to submit to him again!" Wives need to resist these thoughts and remind themselves that they were still right for submitting.

What else should a wife do when her husband makes the wrong decision? More importantly, what should the husband do?

How Husbands Should Respond

When a husband makes the wrong decision, he should acknowledge his mistake without making excuses. If he wants to be his wife's hero, he should admit, "You were right, and I was wrong." If he deliberately did not listen to his wife out of pride or stubbornness, he should also say: "I am sorry. Will you please forgive me? I was being prideful and stubborn."

When a husband acknowledges he made a mistake, it does several things:

1. It blesses his wife.
2. It encourages his wife to submit to him in the future.
3. It sets a good example for his wife and children. Husbands do not lead only by making decisions for the family. They also lead by the example they set.

In Chapter 9, we discussed how husbands end up with the wives they prepare for themselves:

- If husbands make excuses, justify themselves, or blame their wives or children, they very likely may end up with wives—and children—who follow their example and make excuses, justify themselves, and blame others.
- If husbands humble themselves, accept responsibility for their actions, admit when they are wrong, and—maybe most importantly—ask for forgiveness, this will encourage wives and children to accept responsibility for their actions, admit when they are wrong, and ask for forgiveness.

Let me give a personal example. When Katie and I first moved to Washington from California, I decided to rent our house to a woman we knew. Katie told me: "Do not rent to that woman. She is not going to take care of our home." I rented to her anyway, and soon she invited her boyfriend to move in with her. Even though they were not supposed to have pets, they ended up with eight dogs and four cats. The neighbors on both sides started calling me in Washington to complain about the barking and garbage. I received letters from the city threatening to fine me if the messes outside were not cleaned up.

When the woman's lease was up, Katie said, "Thank God she'll finally be out." I, however, decided to try to recoup some of our losses by offering the woman another year. Katie thought I was crazy. The realty company who was handling the property advised me to take legal action to have the woman's wages garnished. I chose not to because the woman claimed to be a Christian and Scripture forbids taking fellow believers to court (1 Corinthians 6:5–7). Since no rent meant no income for the realty company, they were upset with me too. By the time the woman, her children, her boyfriend, and their animals moved out, my house was trashed. I had lost thousands of dollars in rent, and I had to pay thousands of dollars in repairs to get it ready to rent again.

There were lots of excuses I could have given Katie to justify my actions: "She was a family friend and single mother. I wanted to help her. There was no way to know this would happen (even though my wife seemed to know!)." Ultimately, though, there was only one correct response: "You were right, and I was wrong."

How Wives Should Not Respond

Some balance is required. If a husband considers his wife's thoughts, is prayerful, and makes the decision he believes is best for his family, does he need to ask for forgiveness if it turns out to be a mistake? Does he really need to feel as though he did something terrible because a decision he thought was best for his family turned out to be wrong? No. Additionally, wives may be tempted to respond with those four little words: "I told you so!" Whether they come from a wife, husband, child, parent, pastor, friend, etc., those words are always fleshly, prideful, and obnoxious.

The reality is that when husbands make a wrong decision, more than likely they already feel bad enough about it. What a husband really needs is his wife's encouragement and grace. When a husband has the humility to admit he was wrong, a godly wife should say, "Thank you for saying that. We all make mistakes. You did what you thought was best."

Now, obviously, some husbands do not have the humility to admit they have made the wrong decision. Even then a wife should not tell her husband: "I told you so." Instead, she should pray for God to convict her husband and grant him humility and repentance.

Let me also illustrate this point with a situation from my own marriage. When I was teaching elementary school, I learned of another position that would allow me to take better financial care of my family. Driving to the interview, I prayed God would let me receive the job if that was best. Before I left the interview, they offered me the position, which I took as confirmation that this was God's will.

The one drawback of accepting the job was that I lost my secure, tenured position at my current district. Soon after, the recession hit, districts began cutting new teachers, and though I had been teaching almost ten years, I was laid off. I had to go home and tell my pregnant wife that I had lost not only my job but our wonderful medical insurance. You can imagine I was feeling terrible about myself and my decision-making. I even felt frustrated with God for letting me receive a job that I would lose so quickly.

At this low point, here is what Katie could have said: "You had a good, secure teaching position. Why didn't you stick with that? You supposedly prayed about this? Next time, pray a little harder! You're supposed to be the spiritual leader of our family, and your prayers end up with you unemployed? You're supposed to provide for our family, but you don't have a job or insurance?"

Here is how Katie responded instead: "I am so excited to see what God is going to do!"

Katie was right. God did have a plan. This is when Grace Baptist, the church where I was working part-time, decided to hire me full-time. Even though they stepped out in faith because the budget did not support me, the church grew and the annual giving exceeded expenses. I will always remember the way God provided and the way Katie supported me. That is what I needed more than anything else. My wife not only did not make me feel worse about my decision but was a constant encouragement to me.

Chapter Eighteen

A Husband Treats His Wife Well By . . .

1 Peter 3:7—Husbands, likewise, dwell with [your wives]
with understanding, giving honor to the wife, as to the weaker
vessel, and as being heirs together of the grace of life, that your
prayers may not be hindered.

In the first six verses of 1 Peter 3, we looked at the description of a godly wife. Now in verse 7, we find a corresponding description of the way a godly husband should live with his wife. Peter commands wives to submit to their husbands, and then he instructs husbands regarding the treatment of their wives to prevent any abuses of the authority God has given them. Let's begin with a look at the Greek words Peter chose to admonish husbands.

Earlier we discussed the different Greek words for love, and there are also different Greek words for "know" or "knowing." *Epistamai* means "to put one's attention on or to fix one's thoughts on." This is an intellectual knowledge that comes by perceiving or observing, but there is no personal relationship or experience. On the other hand, *ginosko* means "to learn, get a knowledge of, feel." This is a knowledge that comes from personal experience or relationship. Here are two examples:

183

1. I know what rugby is even though I have never played it; therefore, I know it intellectually or *epistamai*. On the other hand, I have played football for years, which means I know it experientially or *ginosko*.

2. I know of (*epistamai*) Abraham Lincoln historically, but I know (*ginosko*) my wife Katie relationally.

Husbands are told to "dwell with [their wives] with understanding," and the word for "understanding" is *gnosis*, related to the word *ginosko*. It describes such a close intimacy that the same word is used in Luke 1:34 when Mary said to the angel who told her she would give birth to the Messiah: "How can this be, since I do not know (*ginosko*) a man?"

Peter commands husbands to develop an intimate knowledge or understanding of their wives that comes through personal experience or relationship. We talked earlier about a wife's learning her husband, understanding just what his needs and strengths are in order to be a "comparable helper." Similarly, husbands need to study their wives and learn them.

Do wives want husbands who make "learning" them a priority? Definitely! Wives feel loved by being understood. A lot of wives wish their husbands knew as much about them as they know about sports, cars, television shows, friends, food, music, video games, you name it. What exactly are husbands supposed to know about their wives? What they like and what they do not like. What is important to them. What they desire and enjoy. A husband ought to know as much as there is to know about the woman he will be with for the rest of his life.

Living with Her According to Knowledge

The word "dwell," or most translations say "live," communicates being together physically, but it means more than just occupying the same house. It refers to a husband's making his wife his lifelong companion. Putting the words "dwell" and "understanding" together, the apostle Peter commands husbands to develop knowledge of their wives and then live with them according to that knowledge:

- A husband should take what he has learned about his wife and apply that knowledge (or "understanding") to their daily lives together.
- A husband should understand how his wife feels loved and seek to love her that way.
- A husband should have knowledge of how his wife wants to be treated and strive to treat her that way.

Katie has given me permission to share two ways she appreciates me "[dwelling] with [her] with understanding" based on the knowledge I have of her:

1. My wife is a visionary, creative woman with lots of plans and thoughts. She likes to think months, years, or even decades down the road. On the other hand, I generally have one focus each week—making sure Sunday goes well. I count time by the number of days until the Lord's Day arrives. When Sunday is over, the countdown begins again. I rarely think eight days ahead (much less eight months or eight years). As a result, Katie appreciates it when I listen to her ideas no matter how far they are in the future, and regardless of whether there is much chance they will come to fruition.

2. Most strengths have a corresponding weakness, so even though Katie has lots of plans, she also has trouble finishing things she starts. Some of her favorite words to say to herself come from Ecclesiastes 7:8: "The end of a thing is better than its beginning." In other words: Finishing is better than starting. Because Katie knows this about herself, she has asked me to do two things for her: encourage her to finish things she starts and discourage her from starting new things until previous things are completed.

These are simple ways Katie wants me to "dwell with [her] with understanding." Each wife is different, which means each husband has to learn his own wife. While this might not be easy, God commands it, which means it is something every husband can and should do. Men should keep in mind that as much as wives are commanded to submit to their husbands, husbands are told to make every effort to *ginosko* their wives and thus to learn—or have an understanding of—them and to live with them according to that knowledge.

Valuing Her Femininity

Peter says to "[give] honor to the wife" and the word for "honor" is *time*. It means "a valuing by which the price is fixed." Eight times in Scripture, *time* is translated as "price" because it refers to the value of something. Here are two examples of its use:

- Matthew 27:6—The chief priests took the silver pieces and said, "It is not lawful to put them into the treasury, because they are the price (*time*) of blood."
- Acts 5:3—Peter said, "Ananias, why has Satan filled your heart to lie to the Holy Spirit and keep back part of the price (*time*) of the land for yourself?"

Peter's message to husbands is clear: Recognize the value of your wife and honor her as a result.

The phrase "to the wife" has an interesting application as well. The Greek word for "wife" is *gyne*, occurring two hundred twenty-one times in the New Testament. The word is used twice in 1 Peter 3: "Wives (*gyne*), likewise, be submissive . . . In former times, the holy women (*gyne*) . . ." (1, 5). But the phrase "to the wife" is only one word in Greek, *gynaikeios*, and this is the only place it occurs in Scripture. While *gyne* is a noun, *gynaikeios* is an adjective meaning "of or belonging to a woman, feminine, female."

Peter is not commanding husbands to honor their wives simply for the sake of honoring them. Instead, husbands are commanded to find value in their wives' femininity and praise them for it. Ladies, young or old, single or married, should celebrate their femininity and enjoy the beauty God has given them.

Protecting Her

Peter says wives are "the weaker vessel" but this does not mean morally, intellectually, or spiritually. Some women are stronger than their husbands in these areas. This is speaking of women's being weaker physically. The Amplified Bible says, "honoring the woman as [physically] the weaker vessel." It is also important to notice that it says "weaker" instead of "weak." Men are physically weak, too. They get sick. They can be injured. They are susceptible to age and eventually die. A man's physical weakness should be a reminder to him to be sensitive to his wife's physical weakness.

Why did God make men physically stronger? He did this for one simple reason—so men can protect women. Husbands should not only protect their wives and daughters but teach their sons to protect other women, especially their sisters and mother. One of the evilest tragedies is when men use their strength to hurt women. Because God gave men greater strength so they could be protective, when a man physically abuses a woman, he is doubly sinning:

- He is committing a sin of commission through his behavior.
- He is committing a sin of omission by failing to use his strength for the reason God gave it to him.

Treating our wives as the weaker vessels means making our wives feel safe and protected. Colossians 3:19 instructs: "Husbands, love your wives and *do not be harsh with them*" (NIV, ESV). Wives should not have to fear verbal, emotional, or physical abuse. It is the husband's responsibility to deal with conflict or danger. Every husband, as best as he can, should put himself between his wife and anything that might threaten her physically, mentally, emotionally, or spiritually.

Even though women are "weaker," with the words "heirs together of the grace of life," Peter prevents his readers from thinking wives are at all inferior to their husbands. The word "heirs" speaks of equality. It reminds a husband that even though he has more authority, his wife is still identical to him in terms of spiritual privilege and importance. A husband should see his wife as a sister in Christ, recognizing that he is married to a daughter of the King who is as much an heir as he is.

Keeping His Prayers from Being "Chopped Down"

First Peter 3:7 ends with a sobering warning that should motivate any husband to treat his wife well: "that your prayers may not be hindered." Scripture teaches that sin can prevent God from hearing us:

- Isaiah 1:15—When you spread out your hands, I will hide My eyes from you; even though you make many prayers, I will not hear. Your hands are full of blood.
- Psalm 66:18—If I regard iniquity in my heart, the Lord will not hear.
- John 9:31—We know that God does not hear sinners; but if anyone is a worshiper of God and does His will, He hears him.

Peter specifies one particular sin that prevents God from hearing the prayers of husbands—the sin of mistreating their wives. The Greek word for "hindered" is *ekkopto*, which means "cut off; of a tree." The Amplified Bible says: "in order that your prayers may not be hindered and cut off." Jesus twice used the word regarding cutting down a fruit tree:

- Matthew 7:19—"Every tree that does not bear good fruit is cut down (*ekkopto*)."
- Luke 13:7—"Look, for three years I have come seeking fruit on this fig tree and find none. Cut it down (*ekkopto*)."

Why would God use the same word for cutting down a fruit tree to describe a husband's prayers being hindered? The intended image is of a husband's prayers being fruitless or "chopped down." A necessity for every husband to be a good spiritual leader is having God hear his prayers, and it is so important to God that husbands treat their wives well that He says He will not hear them if they disobey in this area. The only prayer

God will hear from husbands when they mistreat their wives is a prayer of repentance: "I am very sorry for the way I treated my wife." I am ashamed to say there have been times I have left for the office only to have to turn around and head home to make sure things are right with Katie. I knew I had not treated her the way I should and when I arrived at my office to pray God would not hear me.

The nineteenth century preacher Charles Spurgeon said, "To true believers prayer is so invaluable that the danger of hindering it is used by Peter as a motive . . . in their marriage relationships."[25] Sadly some men have such a low regard for prayer that this warning does not cause them to treat their wives any differently. One reason this attitude is so terrible is that the passage is largely about wives submitting to their husbands, and wives will have a much easier time submitting to spiritual men who are fearful of having their prayers hindered. When a wife has a husband who values having his prayers heard by God more than almost anything else, she will have a much easier time submitting to him as the previous verses described. It would not be too much to say that one of the best ways for a husband to treat his wife well is by keeping his prayers from being "chopped down."

A Husband Mistreats His Wife
When He Responds in Anger

We discussed how husbands should treat their wives, and now we will look at two examples of men who show husbands how *not* to treat their wives.

Jacob married two sisters, Rachel and Leah (Genesis 29:15–28), which in itself was part of the problem. You may ask why biblical patriarchs were allowed to have multiple wives, but polygamy in the Old Testament is descriptive, not prescriptive. It portrays the reality of that era but is not

---

[25] C. H. Spurgeon, *Sermons of the Rev. C.H. Spurgeon, of London, Volume 20* (Sheldon, Blakeman, 1875), p. 506.

allowed for Christians today. We do not see God condoning polygamy, and whenever it took place in the Old Testament, it always caused serious problems. No biblical examples of polygamy are characterized by peace and harmony but rather by turmoil and strife.

Rachel was the more beautiful of the two sisters, and Jacob loved her the most (Genesis 29:17–20, 30). Seeing Jacob's lack of love for Leah, however, God opened her womb and gave her a total of six sons and at least one daughter (Genesis 29:31–35). In that era, being infertile was a great shame for a woman, so you can imagine how Rachel was feeling. Genesis 30:1 says, "Now when Rachel saw that she bore Jacob no children, Rachel envied her sister, and said to Jacob, 'Give me children, or else I die!'"

This account is instructive not only for husbands but for wives as well. Not having any children might be terrible, but talking of dying because of it was rather melodramatic. Second, consider whom Rachel holds responsible for her suffering—her husband. Was it really Jacob's fault that she could not have any children? Clearly not since he had been able to have children with Leah. Instead of blaming Jacob, Rachel should have taken her problem in prayer to God.

Here is the application for wives:

- When you are suffering, do you hold your husband responsible?
- When you are upset, do you get upset with your husband?
- When you are having a bad day, do you make sure your husband— or the rest of your family—has a bad day, too?

Going back to Rachel, much of her anger stemmed from her sister Leah's having children. Her anger was not motivated by something her husband had done but by her own sins: jealousy and discontentment. A wife reading this could ask herself: "Am I jealous of other women? Do I covet what they have? Am I discontent with my lot in life? Is it planting a root of bitterness in my heart as it did with Rachel?"

Even so, Jacob had the opportunity to be a loving, sensitive husband. If he was familiar with the principle of 1 Peter 3:7, he should ask himself:

"How can I dwell with my wife with understanding? How can I give honor to her, recognizing she is the weaker vessel? Part of her femininity is a desire to have children, so she has a reason to be upset. We are heirs together of the grace of life, so how would God have me treat her right now so my prayers will not be hindered? I know what I will say: 'I am so sorry you have not been able to have any children. This must be really difficult. Let's pray about this together.'"

Instead, Genesis 30:2 tells us: "And Jacob's anger was aroused against Rachel, and he said, 'Am I in the place of God, who has withheld from you the fruit of the womb?'" Other versions translate this even more strongly: "Jacob's anger was kindled" (ESV). "Jacob's anger burned" (NASB).

Jacob's words were true enough; he was not in control of whether his wife conceived and had children. But he was still wrong because of the way he responded. When wives are upset and emotional, it can be tempting for husbands to get angry in return, but God commands us to dwell with our wives with understanding. A husband should consider why his wife is upset, show her compassion, and then pray with her and for her.

A Husband Mistreats His Wife When He Responds in Pride

Elkanah also had two wives, Hannah and Peninnah. Similar to Jacob and his wives, Peninnah could have children, and Hannah could not, but what made Hannah's situation even worse was Peninnah's cruelty toward her. First Samuel 1:6–7 records:

> [Hannah's] rival (Peninnah) provoked her severely, to make her miserable, because the LORD had closed her womb. So it was, year by year, when she went up to the house of the LORD, that [Peninnah] provoked her; therefore [Hannah] wept and did not eat.

There is a difference and a similarity between Jacob and Elkanah. The difference is that while Jacob responded in anger, Elkanah tried to cheer his wife up. The similarity is that, in the process, Elkanah ended up being as insensitive as Jacob. First Samuel 1:8 records: "Then Elkanah her husband said to her, 'Hannah, why do you weep? Why do you not eat? And why is your heart grieved? Am I not better to you than ten sons?'"

Husbands, when your wife is upset, do not use Elkanah as a model! In this one verse he made three common mistakes:

1. He asked insensitive questions that gave the impression that his wife's hurt was not legitimate. He knew good and well why she felt this way—because she was unable to have children.

2. He tried to cheer Hannah up. Proverbs 25:20 says, "Like one who takes away a garment in cold weather, and like vinegar on soda, is one who sings songs to a heavy heart." Husbands should respond sympathetically by listening well and then saying, "I am so sorry. What can I do for you? Would you like me to pray for you?"

3. He made the king of all prideful statements: "Is not being married to me better than all the children you could have?" What does it look like today for husbands to be like this? "You are one lucky lady. Think of all I do for you! Aren't you glad you get to be married to me?"

Jacob and Elkanah are husbands who really did not understand their wives, as their terrible responses when Rachel and Hannah were grieving demonstrate. Husbands, when our wives are upset, let's make sure we do not respond to them in anger because we lack patience or in pride by telling them all the wonderful things we have done for them. These are both ways to ensure that we are disobeying 1 Peter 3:7.

Part VII: I Corinthians 7:1–6

A Biblical View of Intimacy

Chapter Nineteen

The Case for Intimacy

Hebrews 13:4—Marriage is honorable among all, and the bed undefiled; but fornicators and adulterers God will judge.

Sexual intimacy is not neglected in Scripture, as it is discussed a number of times in the Old and New Testaments. One entire book—Song of Solomon—is dedicated largely to the topic. When God's Word makes something important, Christians have a responsibility to make it important as well by learning what Scripture teaches on the subject. If Christians do not do this, they are likely to gain their understanding from secular society, which has a perverse view of sexuality. So let's take a closer look at God's intended design for intimacy between a husband and wife.

Understanding *Eros*

Recall that the original Greek language in which the New Testament was written used various words for love—*phileo, storge, agape,* and *eros.* Eros is the type of love specifically related to sexual intimacy between husband and wife.

One of the major principles we discussed earlier is that love is not so much an emotion as an action. Love is patient, love is kind, etc. (1 Corinthians 13); that is, love is what love does. In contrast, *eros* is exactly the opposite. It is not a demonstration of loving action toward someone as much as it is a feeling. Specifically, it describes the sensation people

experience when they are physically attracted to someone. The word *eros* is the root of the English word *erotic*.

While the actual word *eros* does not occur in Scripture, we can most definitely see the principle behind it. *Eros* is what Samson felt in Judges 14:2 when he told his parents: "I have seen a woman in Timnah of the daughters of the Philistines; now therefore, get her for me as a wife." *Eros* is how King David found himself in the worst trouble of his life when he stepped out on his rooftop and spotted "[Bathsheba] bathing, and the woman was very beautiful to behold" (2 Samuel 11:2). Song of Solomon gives a clear depiction of *eros* as it describes the strong physical attraction the man and woman feel toward each other.

Eros is self-centered in that it relates to the way a person feels and what a person wants. No thought or consideration is given to the object of one's *eros*. *Eros* will not move a person to be forgiving, sacrificial, or kind, which is why it is so important not to base a marriage on *eros*. Many couples have wanted to get married because of strong feelings of *eros* for each other, but when the *eros* eventually wears off, they find themselves frustrated and uninterested.

That, of course, is the problem with *eros:* It can wear off. It can change with certain things such as time, age, or physical appearance. When *eros* is the foundation of a relationship, couples often find out their relationship had no real foundation at all. If a relationship is based on *eros* alone, then when *eros* is gone, the relationship is also gone. For a true lasting relationship, the thrill and excitement of *eros* must be supported by a deeper, unchanging love and commitment. It must be based on the other types of love we discussed earlier—the sacrificial love of *agape* and the abiding affection and friendship of *phileo*.

To be clear, *eros* is not immoral or sinful. In fact, it is an important part of marriages. It is the attraction husbands and wives should feel for each other. If we lack *eros* for our spouses, there are two things we can do:

1. We should rip our eyes away from anything that provokes feelings of *eros* for anyone other than our spouses. We should do this

because God commands it as part of living a holy life, but we should also understand that failing to do so destroys the *eros* in marriage. Individuals who give themselves over to pornography or lust find very quickly that they have no *eros* for their spouses.

2. We should always go to Scripture with life's problems, and we can find the answer to an absence of *eros* in the Song of Solomon. This book helps husbands and wives enjoy the physical aspects of marriage. As you read it, pray for God to restore and increase your *eros* for your spouse. It is a wonderful prayer request.

Intimacy in Marriage Is Blessed by God

Just as the devil has been successful in encouraging intimacy outside of marriage, I have discovered in years of marriage counseling that he has been equally successful in discouraging intimacy within marriage. I once counseled a man in his fifties who was addicted to pornography. I mention his age only because pornography might be more typically considered a struggle for young, single men. In reality it can enslave men—and women as well—of any age, in any season of life.

The man's actions were absolutely sinful; there is no minimizing the wickedness of his behavior. With that said, after months of counseling it became apparent that one reason for his addiction was a wrong view of intimacy. His mother had convinced him at a young age that sex was filthy, and he had never been able to rid himself of that belief. He told me: "I look at porn, because at least then I am not involving my wife in a dirty activity." Though I tried to convince him otherwise, it was very difficult for him to shake his mother's teaching.

I share this story because this man is far from the only person I have met who believes that sex in marriage is somehow immoral. Scripture disagrees! In Hebrews 13:4 the words "the bed" are a euphemism for sexual activity, and within marriage God calls it "undefiled" or pure. It is the same Greek word used earlier in Hebrews 7:26 to describe Jesus, our High Priest, as "holy, harmless, *undefiled*." God wants us to know there is absolutely nothing sinful or immoral about sexual activity between a husband and wife.

In the Song of Solomon the couple consummate their relationship in Chapter 4, and it is followed by God's approval in 5:1: "Eat, O friends! Drink, yes, drink deeply, O beloved ones!" This invitation is meant to encourage husbands and wives in their sexual activity. Not only should intimacy in marriage *not* be thought of as neutral, amoral, or non-spiritual, it should be thought of as good, spiritual, and blessed by God.

Intimacy in Marriage Is for Enjoyment as Much as Procreation

God's purpose for intimacy goes far beyond simple procreation. Yes, God created sex so couples can fulfill His command in Genesis 1:28 to "be fruitful and multiply," but He also gave intimacy as a gift for our pleasure. The Song of Solomon is filled with passages describing the way the husband and wife enjoy each other physically. Consider these verses:

- Let him kiss me with the kisses of his mouth—
  For your love is better than wine (1:2).
- A bundle of myrrh is my beloved to me,
  That lies all night between my breasts (1:13).
- Like an apple tree among the trees of the woods,
  So is my beloved among the sons.
  I sat down in his shade with great delight,
  And his fruit was sweet to my taste (2:3).
- Your two breasts are like two fawns,
  Twins of a gazelle,
  Which feed among the lilies (4:5).

The verses are discreet but unmistakable in describing the physical pleasure the husband and wife experience. They truly enjoy discovering each other and opening themselves up to each other. Within the marriage relationship there is a sexual liberty and freedom that God wants couples to enjoy.

Intimacy in Marriage Is Commanded

In 1 Corinthians 7:1b–3, the apostle Paul says:

> It is good for a man not to touch a woman. Nevertheless, because
> of sexual immorality, let each man have his own wife, and let each
> woman have her own husband. Let the husband render to his wife
> the affection due her, and likewise also the wife to her husband.

The phrase "touch a woman" is another euphemism for sex. Paul
commands single people to remain celibate but then adds that it is equally
bad for married people to abstain. While we recognize intimacy outside of
marriage is wrong, so we should also recognize that withholding intimacy
in marriage is equally wrong. Paul instructs married people to "render" to
their spouses the "affection" or intimacy that is "due." The Greek word
for "due" is *opheilo*, which means "to owe, be in debt for." Here are two
places it is used:

- Matthew 18:28–30—But that servant went out and found one of
  his fellow servants who owed (*opheilo*) him a hundred denarii; and
  he . . . threw him into prison till he should pay the debt (*opheilo*).
- Luke 7:41—There was a certain creditor who had two debtors. One
  owed (*opheilo*) five hundred denarii, and the other fifty.

Spouses owe affection—or intimacy—to each other. Withholding
intimacy out of anger or to be vindictive or manipulative is not only
unloving but also sinful.

Your Body Belongs to Your Spouse

In the same passage the apostle Paul continues: "The wife does not have
authority over her own body, but the husband does. And likewise the
husband does not have authority over his own body, but the wife does"
(1 Corinthians 7:4). We discussed in previous chapters a husband's
authority in the marriage relationship, so it is significant to see that
regarding intimacy, husbands and wives have equal authority over their
spouses' bodies. This makes sense because when it comes to intimacy, our

goal should be to please our spouses willingly. We should count our bodies not as our own but as belonging to our spouses. Two points regarding this truth:

1. Since your body belongs to your spouse, whatever you do with your body should have the approval of your spouse. For example, if a man wants to have a beard, he should take into consideration whether or not his wife wants him to have one. If a woman wants to wear her hair a certain way, she should take into consideration her husband's thoughts.

2. This is a good reason to take care of yourself. You have to keep in mind that your spouse will enjoy your body for the rest of his or her life. You should make reasonable efforts to stay healthy so you can be a blessing to your spouse, be around for a long number of years, and be available to take care of your spouse if he or she becomes sick.

Should You Ever Abstain?

The Old Testament discussed circumstances during which people should abstain from sexual activity. When the Israelites gathered at Mount Sinai to receive the Ten Commandments, they were commanded to abstain as part of their preparations to meet God (Exodus 19:10–14). A more ordinary period of abstinence took place after a woman gave birth. She was considered unclean for seven days following the birth of a son and two weeks following the birth of a girl (Leviticus 12:1–5). A similar restriction of seven days occurred when a woman was menstruating (Leviticus 15:19–24, 18:19, 20:18). The original purpose of these verses is found in an understanding of the sacredness of blood in the Old Testament: "For the life of the flesh is in the blood, and I have given it to you upon the altar to make atonement for your souls; for it is the blood that makes atonement for the soul" (Leviticus 17:11). Forbidding contact with a menstruating woman revealed the value placed on blood.

The obvious question is: Should husbands and wives abstain today as a result of these Old Testament commands? Some couples choose to abstain because they believe these commands have an ongoing application. Others feel the ceremonial portions of the Law—under which these commands fall—are no more binding than the commands to offer blood sacrifices. Romans 14:5 provides some latitude for couples as they address these types of questions: "Let each be fully convinced in his own mind." Couples should agree together regarding the circumstances under which they choose to abstain. Unless both husband and wife agree to abstain, then they should not abstain. This is supported by the apostle Paul's words as he continues his instruction in 1 Corinthians 7:5–6:

> Do not deprive one another *except with consent* for a time, that you may give yourselves to fasting and prayer; and come together again so that Satan does not tempt you because of your lack of self-control. But I say this as a concession, not as a commandment.

Even when the New Testament discusses abstinence, it is for the purposes of "fasting and prayer," as opposed to observing Old Testament commands. Paul also makes the point that couples do not have to abstain. He was simply saying they can if they choose to for the reasons mentioned. If a husband and wife go their entire marriage without ever abstaining that is perfectly acceptable. If they do abstain, the words "for a time" and "come together again" mean the abstinence should be for a determined, limited season. The words "so that Satan does not tempt you" reveal the reason: There is greater potential for temptation while abstaining. In 1 Corinthians 7:9 Paul wrote, "But if they cannot exercise self-control, let them marry. For it is better to marry than to burn with passion." First Corinthians 7:5 and 1 Corinthians 7:9 both teach that when people are without physical intimacy their self-control is tested, and for that reason abstinence should be for a limited time.

Husbands and wives must recognize that when they deprive their spouses, they are putting them in a spiritually precarious situation. They are making the spouse feel, once again, like a single person "[burning] with passion." A man or woman who looks at pornography or commits adultery cannot blame the sin and lack of self-control on the spouse, but it is important to understand that husbands and wives who withhold affection are subjecting their spouses to greater temptation. With that knowledge, combined with the teaching that their bodies belong to their spouses, how committed should they be to satisfying their husbands or wives—not just to obey God's commands but to help their spouses avoid temptation?

Chapter Twenty

When Intimacy Is Threatened

As discussed in the previous chapter, God gave us sex as a gift. The problem, though, is that as sinful people in a fallen world, we have the potential to ruin anything good God gives us. Let's take a look at three of the most common threats to healthy intimacy in marriage.

Threatened by Selfish Attitudes

Husbands and wives should be committed to satisfying each other, but Scripture must also be balanced in light of other Scripture. If 1 Corinthians 7 were the only passage considered, people could demand their spouses satisfy their desires regardless of the way the other person feels, but we have looked at other passages—such as Ephesians 5 and 1 Peter 3—that mandate love, gentleness, compassion, and deference in the marriage relationship. While it would be unhealthy and even sinful to deprive our spouses for selfish reasons, it can also be equally unhealthy and sinful to be demanding or insensitive toward our spouses.

Although Paul listed fasting and prayer as possible reasons for abstinence, common sense and simple consideration dictate there are other acceptable reasons—sickness, pregnancy, or grief. At times when people are suffering or struggling, they might find intimacy terribly unattractive. God wants sex to be enjoyable for both individuals. Selfish and unkind attitudes threaten the joy and pleasure God desires for couples.

Threatened by Mismatched Desires

Because no two people are the same, marriages always involve a number of differences that have the potential to cause problems—finances, parenting, organization, promptness. Among these differences are mismatched desires for physical intimacy. There will inevitably be times when one spouse desires sex and the other does not. Possibly causing even more tension, there can be different desires regarding how the actual physical intimacy itself takes place.

Since sex should be enjoyable for both spouses, couples should strive to ensure there is a mutual level of comfort regarding expressions of intimacy. Love and respect means caring how the other person feels.

Let me present a situation that can happen in any marriage. Spouse A desires intimacy while Spouse B does not. While there are no contradictions in Scripture, there can be situations when biblical commands would appear to compete with each other. For example:

- Spouse A might quote from 1 Corinthians 7 that spouses should not deprive each other, perhaps even being insensitive enough to add: "I know you don't want to do this, but I don't care. You need to obey God and recognize your body belongs to me like Paul said!"
- Spouse B might then respond: "Why don't you flip forward a few chapters and read about love in 1 Corinthians 13! And Philippians 2 says you're not supposed to look out for your own interests but to esteem others above yourself!"

So, should Spouse A's desire for physical intimacy be satisfied or Spouse B's desire for no physical intimacy? We have already discussed how God established a husband's headship and a wife's submission in order to break a stalemate so the relationship can go forward. We have also discussed from 1 Corinthians 7:4 that husbands and wives have equal authority over each other's bodies. As a result, unlike most impasses in marriage, it is not as easy as simply going with the husband's decision. For lack of a better way to say it: "Who wins?"

Boiling conflict down to who wins is not only selfish but will always cause problems. When counseling, I try to avoid being a referee. That makes marriage look like a competition, with husbands and wives seeing themselves on opposing teams competing against each other. This could not be further from what God desires when He joins two people together and makes them one flesh.

Rather than winning, a better approach for each spouse is one that seeks to die to self and please the other. If both spouses have this attitude:

- Spouse A will appreciate the effort Spouse B makes to satisfy Spouse A's desire for intimacy even when Spouse B does not want to be intimate.
- Spouse B will appreciate when Spouse A puts Spouse B's feelings ahead of Spouse A's desires.

This approach allows couples to have a strong relationship and, more often than not, differences of mismatched desires will resolve themselves.

One might think that the "best" marriages exist between two people almost identical in every way, but even the most compatible couple will have a miserable marriage if they are selfish. The healthiest, most joyful relationships consist of people who are the most giving, selfless, and sacrificial. This applies to every area of marriage, including intimacy. With that said, let me add two important disclaimers:

1. If I had to suggest erring on one side or the other, I would recommend erring on the side of satisfying your spouse. Why? First Corinthians 7 commands husbands and wives to satisfy each other, but there are no competing Scriptures telling believers that they do not have to satisfy their spouses. Yes, we have considered biblical instruction regarding being loving, compassionate, and considerate toward our spouses, but those verses do not relate directly to intimacy. We have direct commands to please our spouses, but any verses we might think give us an out from pleasing our spouses must instead be inferred. A direct command

should always carry more weight than verses that require inferences.

2. Consider the results of both courses of action. The potential consequences of not satisfying your spouse far outweigh the "consequences"—if you want to call it that—of satisfying your spouse. There are not many drawbacks to pleasing your husband or wife, but the apostle Paul said that when people go without physical intimacy they are subjected to greater temptation (1 Corinthians 7:5).

Threatened by Impurity

Of all the gifts God has given us, sex might be the most perverted. This is even more tragic when we consider that intimacy is most enjoyed when couples have pure hearts and minds. People who reserve all of their desires and passions for their spouses will have the healthiest sex lives, and this is why impurity is one of the greatest threats to intimacy.

In any discussion of impurity, pornography almost immediately comes to mind. My son Ricky recently shared with me how amazed he was that a bull can be controlled by a ring through its nose. He could not believe that a creature so big and powerful could be led around by something as small and insignificant as a ring. This is what pornography does with people. It controls them. It does not matter how powerful or significant people are, when they introduce pornography into their lives, it will control them.

We also have to be concerned with what we set our hearts, thoughts, or feelings on. While there is nothing wrong with having friendships between genders, we should be cautious of becoming too close with those of the opposite sex. Even if your feelings for someone are pure and healthy, you cannot control how someone may feel towards you, and you do not want to become the object of someone else's misplaced affection.

It is best to err on the side of caution and avoid becoming "the good listener" or "shoulder to lean on" for a friend of the opposite sex. This is especially true with married friends who should be pursuing such relationships with their spouses. Recently I have learned of three prominent ministry leaders who experienced moral failures because of their relationships with the opposite sex. More than likely each situation began with casual friendships that escalated after becoming too close.

Much of this has to do with contentment. Many in secular society view contentment as they view love—as a feeling or emotion over which they have no control. The Bible, however, presents contentment the same way it presents love—as a decision. In marriage we choose to be content or discontent with our spouses—the way our spouses look and what our spouses offer us. This is illustrated in Proverbs 5:18–19:

> Let your fountain be blessed,
> And rejoice with the wife of your youth.
> As a loving deer and a graceful doe,
> Let her breasts satisfy you at all times;
> And always be enraptured with her love.

A number of words reveal the pleasure God wants us to experience with our spouses: "blessed . . . satisfy . . . enraptured." We have the choice to feel these ways toward our spouses, and that is communicated by the words, "Rejoice . . . Let her satisfy you at all times . . . always be enraptured with her." These words are commands we can obey or disobey. Husbands and wives can choose to be content with their spouses, but only if they are pure.

The couple in Song of Solomon only had eyes and feelings for each other. They were completely content with each other. As a result, their physical intimacy was healthy and joyful.

Part VIII: Matthew 7:24–27

A Strong Foundation

Chapter Twenty-One

Building on Christ

Matthew 7:24—Therefore whoever hears these sayings of Mine, and does them, I will liken him to a wise man who built his house on the rock.

The Old Testament looked forward to Jesus:

- Luke 24:27—And beginning at Moses and all the Prophets, [Jesus] expounded to them in all the Scriptures the things *concerning Himself.*
- John 5:39—[Jesus said], "You search the Scriptures . . . and these are they which *testify of Me."*

There are many titles for God in the Old Testament, and the New Testament reveals Jesus as the true and greater fulfillment of them. For example, in the Old Testament God is called:

- Shepherd (Psalm 23:1–4; Ezekiel 34:11–24) and in John 10:11 Jesus said: "I am the good shepherd. The good shepherd gives His life for the sheep."
- Redeemer (Psalm 19:14; Isaiah 41:14) and Galatians 3:13a says, "Christ has redeemed us from the curse of the law."
- Deliverer (2 Samuel 22:2; Psalm 144:2) and 1 Thessalonians 1:10 says, "Jesus . . . delivers us from the wrath to come."
- Judge (Genesis 18:25; Ezekiel 34:17) and in John 5:22 Jesus said, "The Father . . . has committed all judgment to the Son."

- The strength of His people (Psalm 18:1; Psalm 28:7) and in Philippians 4:13 Paul said he "can do all things through Christ who strengthens [him]."

There are plenty of other titles for God that have their fulfillment in Jesus, but one is particularly relevant to our discussion. "Rock" is a common Old Testament title for God:

- Deuteronomy 32:4a—He is the Rock, His work is perfect.
- 1 Samuel 2:2b—Nor is there any rock like our God.
- Psalm 144:1a—Blessed be the LORD my Rock.

In the New Testament this title finds its fulfillment in Jesus. In 1 Corinthians 10:4, the apostle Paul identifies Christ as the Rock that was with Israel in the wilderness: "They drank of that spiritual Rock that followed them, and that rock was Christ." Jesus was there providing spiritually for the nation of Israel as they traveled to the Promised Land.

Jesus is also the Rock for the church. In Matthew 16:18 Jesus told Peter, "On this rock I will build My church." Though the verse is a play on Peter's name, which means "rock," Jesus was not referring to Peter himself but to Peter's profession of faith in Christ and the way the church would be a group of people with that same profession.

In construction when a rock serves as the foundation for a building, it receives a special name—cornerstone. The New Testament identifies Jesus as the Rock the church is built on:

- Acts 4:11—The 'stone which was rejected . . . has become the chief cornerstone.'
- Ephesians 2:20b—Jesus Christ Himself being the chief cornerstone.
- 1 Peter 2:6—Behold, I lay in Zion a chief cornerstone.

Just as Jesus was the Rock for Israel and is the Rock for the church, He can also be the Rock—or foundation—for our marriages. In Matthew 7:24–27 Jesus discussed a wise man who built his house on a strong foundation of rock and a foolish man who built on a foundation of sand.

The Greek word for "house" is *oikia*, and it can refer to a physical dwelling or a family or household. For our purposes, think specifically of a married couple.

I would like to conclude our journey together discussing these builders for two reasons:

1. Jesus brought the Sermon on the Mount to a close with this teaching. He wanted to make sure His listeners put into practice what they heard. My prayer is that you will put into practice what you have read.

2. This teaching makes clear that there is only one true foundation for healthy, joyful relationships: Jesus Christ.

The Storms Will Come

Why is it so important to have a strong foundation? Jesus said, "and the rain descended, the floods came, and the winds blew and beat on that house" (Matthew 7:25a). These storms represent the trials of life. You have probably seen on the news—or perhaps personally experienced—what can happen to a house under the onslaught of a hurricane, tornado, or tsunami. Jesus was not teaching that the weather will be unpleasant or chilly and people might need an umbrella or coat. He was describing storms that have the potential to destroy a house, illustrating the potential trials have to destroy a marriage.

Furthermore, Jesus did not present the rain, floods, and winds as possibilities that only some couples will be unfortunate enough to experience. He said, "the rain descended, the floods came, and the winds blew." The storms are inevitable. It is certain that couples will experience trials:

- James 1:2—Count it all joy *when* you fall into various trials.
- Acts 14:22—We *must* through many tribulations enter the kingdom of God.
- 1 Thessalonians 3:3—No one should be shaken by these afflictions; for you yourselves know that we *are appointed* to this.

- John 16:33—In the world you *will have* tribulation.
- 1 Peter 4:12—*Do not think it strange* concerning the fiery trial which is to try you, as though some strange thing happened to you.

We do not know when there will be storms, but we do know they will come. They could be a health or financial issue, rebellious child, job loss, or betrayal from a friend. Additionally, they do not have to be large, terrible, life-changing events. The words "beat on that house" refer to the daily struggles that wear on a marriage until a husband and wife feel as though they are going to collapse. At one time or another most married people have said: "I don't think I can do this anymore! I can't make it through one more day."

So let's be clear about what Jesus was not teaching. He was not saying that obeying Him will keep marriages from experiencing storms. Sometimes we think that if we are obedient, then God will not allow us to face trials, but Jesus was describing storms that beat on a house that was built on a strong foundation.

If obeying Jesus's teaching does not enable couples to avoid trials, what benefit is there in building a marriage on Christ? The tremendous promise Jesus made was that His teaching enables relationships to survive even the worst trials: "[the house] did not fall, for it was founded on the rock" (Matthew 7:25b). Although a marriage that obeys Jesus's teachings will not avoid the storms of life, it will survive even the worst trials.

Perhaps you have witnessed a Christian marriage experiencing terrible suffering and thought: "How can they handle that? I don't know what I would do if that were me!" The great encouragement to take away from Jesus's words is that if you are obeying His teaching, you can be assured that you, too, will be able to withstand these same storms.

Chapter Twenty-Two

The Importance of Obeying

Matthew 7:26—But everyone who hears these sayings of
Mine, and does not do them, will be like a foolish man who
built his house on the sand.

When teaching elementary school, I would stand in front of the classroom and explain as clearly as possible what the students were supposed to do. Then I would encourage them to do it on their own. As I walked around the room looking over shoulders, it became evident that although the students received the same instruction, they generally fell into two groups: Some applied what they heard and others did not.

When I coached wrestling I spent part of each practice teaching new moves. I would explain the technique step-by-step and then put the wrestlers in pairs to try it themselves. Again, even though the athletes watched the same demonstration, some put into practice what I taught, while others did not.

Jesus also knew His hearers would fall into one of the same two categories as my students and athletes. Some would hear what He said and apply it, while others would not. The importance of going beyond hearing (or reading) to obeying is a theme in Scripture. Jesus said, "My mother and My brothers are these who hear the word of God *and do it* . . . If you know these things, blessed are you *if you do them*" (Luke 8:21, John 13:17). We do not learn God's Word simply for the sake of knowing it. We learn it so that we can apply it.

James 1:22 says, "But be doers of the word, and not hearers only, deceiving yourselves." This verse reveals a common deception. People learn God's Word and believe they have done enough even though they have not applied it to their lives. Husbands and wives make this same mistake when they believe they have a marriage built on Christ simply because they know what the Bible teaches, even though they are not obeying the instruction. Our responsibility goes much further than simply obtaining information. We have to obey what we have learned.

If you are not building on Christ—which is to say you are not obeying the commands in Scripture—then you should not have much confidence that your marriage will survive the storms of life. This is exactly what Jesus said in Matthew 7:27: "And the rain descended, the floods came, and the winds blew and beat on that house; and it fell. And great was its fall." Jesus's words are strong, but was He being harsh? Just the opposite! He was being gracious and loving. He talked this way to convince His hearers—including us—to have Him as the foundation for their marriages because He knows that is the only way they will remain standing!

Jesus preached the greatest sermon in history, but those who heard and did not obey were no better off than those who never heard the teaching. You have read twenty-one chapters explaining God's commands for marriage, but if you do not obey those commands your marriage will be no different from those who never read this book. Christ is the strong foundation for your marriage, but only if you obey Him.

Response Determines Outcome

The accounts of the wise man and the foolish man are almost identical:

- They both seem to be talented builders.
- There was nothing to indicate any difference in their houses; they achieved the same goal of building a strong, sturdy house.

- They faced the same storms; verses 25 and 27 say, "the rain descended, the floods came, and the winds blew and beat on that house."

This is why the two different outcomes are so shocking: "it did not fall, for it was founded on the rock" versus "it fell. And great was its fall." Nearly identical circumstances, but completely different outcomes. The only difference was the foundation of each house.

Similarly, it is not the marriage itself, nor the amount of trials suffered, that leads to different outcomes for couples. At Woodland Christian Church, we have celebrations for people reaching fifty years of marriage. Did they stay married that long because their marriages were free from troubles? Are we celebrating how God graciously gave them five decades without trials? No! It is not the absence of trials that allows people to stay married for any number of years. It is the foundation. The response to Jesus's teaching—whether a husband and wife choose to build on the Rock—determines whether their house will stand up to life's storms.

Wisdom and Foolishness Is Revealed by What We Do

We typically think of wisdom and foolishness related to knowledge. People are considered wise because they have some measure of knowledge or foolish because they lack knowledge. But this was not the way Jesus defined wisdom and foolishness. In Luke 7:35 He said, "Wisdom is justified by all her children." In other words, wisdom is demonstrated—or shown to be right—by what it produces, and there might be no better example of this than the two builders.

Both builders heard the same teachings of Jesus, which means they had the same knowledge. The wise builder was deemed wise because he applied what he heard, and the foolish builder was deemed foolish because he did not. A good definition of wisdom is, "Using the knowledge we have to do what is right." A good definition of foolishness is, "Having the knowledge to do what is right, but not doing it."

The questions facing your marriage are:

- Are you going to be wise, or are you going to be foolish?
- Are you going to obey the instruction you have learned, or are you going to be foolish and ignore God's commands?
- Are you building your marriage on a strong foundation, or are you building on sand?

Your wisdom or foolishness is not shown by what you know or by how many Christian marriage books you have read. Your wisdom or foolishness is shown by what you do. By the way you live. Whether you obey what you have learned. And having healthy, joyful marriages requires obeying Christ's teaching.

Epilogue

The Mystery of Marriage

*Ephesians 5:30, 32—For we are members of His body, of
His flesh and of His bones. This is a great mystery, but I
speak concerning Christ and the church.*

In Scripture, the word "mystery" refers to something previously
concealed and then later revealed. Ephesians 5:32 speaks of "a great
mystery" that began at the creation of Adam and Eve, was concealed
throughout the Old Testament, and then revealed in the New Testament:
Marriage is a picture of Christ's relationship to the church. It is the mystery
we have discussed throughout the book:

- Just as Adam was Eve's head, so too is Christ our head (Ephesians
  5:23; Colossians 1:18).
- Just as Eve came from Adam's body to be his helper, so too we are
  the body of Christ serving as His "helper" carrying on His work in
  His physical absence (1 Corinthians 12:12–27).
- Just as God put Adam to sleep and created Eve physically from his
  side, so as Jesus slept the sleep of death on the cross and in the
  grave, God created the church spiritually from our wounded Savior.

While Christ had disciples during His earthly ministry, He did not have
a bride until He laid down His life on the cross. An analogy would be a

young man deeply loves a young lady, but until he pledges himself to her she does not become his bride. In the same way, the followers of Jesus did not become His bride until He pledged Himself to them through His death. Then the disciples moved from being followers to being the redeemed bride.

The Love of Christ for His Bride

Consider this: If Adam cared for Eve because she was part of his flesh and his bones, how much better will Christ care for us who are His body, His flesh, and His bones? If you can imagine the love Adam had for Eve, imagine the much greater love that Christ has for us. Husbands are commanded to sacrifice for their brides, but think on the even greater sacrifice Jesus made for His bride.

Paul expressed a desire that the Ephesians, to whom he addressed his marriage passage, would catch a vision of just how much Christ loved them. This is the same desire I have for you as you conclude this marriage book:

> That Christ may dwell in your hearts through faith; that you, being rooted and grounded in love, may be able to comprehend with all the saints what is the width and length and depth and height—to know the love of Christ which passes knowledge; that you may be filled with all the fullness of God (Ephesians 3:17–19).

The Prayers for You

Upon reaching the epilogue I prayed: "Father, a large part of my heart is in this book. What would You have me say to Your readers at the end of this journey?" Soon after this prayer, something painful and discouraging happened. While I cannot give any details, I can share how God comforted me. We live in a parsonage, which is only a few hundred feet from my office. I stood up from behind my desk and decided to walk home. I knew it would take some time before I would be able to resume working as I processed everything that had happened. On the way home I felt hurt and discouraged. The situation weighed heavily on me.

Then something else happened. I reached our home and Katie welcomed me with a smile, a hug, and a kiss. Immediately I felt better. Some of the burden was lifted. Katie had no idea what had just taken place. She did not provide any counsel to make the situation better. Simply being with the bride God gave me changed a situation that was "not good" to "very good" (Genesis 1:31, 2:18).

Well, to be honest, I would not say the situation became very good, but I would say it became better. By evening it was still bothering me. Making things worse, Katie and I were not able to be together that night, but right before I went to bed she sent me a text saying: "Praying for you to rest well tonight, and trust that none of this is a surprise to our Lord. I believe He is able to do great things through all of this. You will always have me by your side cheering you on. Love you. Rest well in trusting Him."

This is the wonderful wife God has given me! It was a blessing to have Katie's love and support throughout that painful situation, but I am convinced that this is not a blessing God wants only for me. This is a blessing God wants for all of us through the gift of marriage.

Living in a sinful, fallen world means experiencing painful situations, but our God is gracious and loving. Knowing what this life holds for us, He has given us marriage so we do not have to go through these trials alone. Aside from such spiritual blessings as salvation, the Scriptures, and the Holy Spirit, the greatest gift God has given us is marriage. Make every effort to see your husband or wife this way—as a gift.

During the time I wrote this book, I prayed for everyone who would read these words. I will continue to pray for you in years to come, but, may it be an even greater encouragement that Jesus is "[making] intercession for [you]" (Romans 8:34). You can be sure that intercession includes your marriage, because it is a depiction to the world around you of Christ's own relationship with His bride. Nobody wants your marriage to reflect the beauty of that divine relationship more than Jesus Himself. And by following the recipe in Scripture, we can have the healthy, joyful, Christ-centered relationships God wants for us.

About the Author

S cott is the senior pastor of Woodland Christian Church in Woodland, Washington and a conference speaker. He and his wife, Katie, grew up together in northern California, and God has blessed them with seven children.

You can contact Pastor Scott or learn more about him at the following:

- Email: scott@scottlapierre.org
- Website: www.scottlapierre.org
- Facebook: @ScottLaPierreAuthor
- YouTube: @ScottLaPierre
- Twitter: @PastorWCC
- Instagram: @PastorWCC

Receive FREE chapters of Pastor Scott's books and videos of his conference messages by subscribing to his newsletter:

www.subscribepage.com/ScottLaPierre

Would you (or your church) like to host a Marriage God's Way Conference?

You can expect:

- Professionally prepared and delivered messages
- Handouts with lessons and discussion questions
- Copies of Pastor Scott's books to offer as gifts to increase registrations (if you desire)
- Prompt replies to communication
- Advertising of your event on Pastor Scott's social media

Schedule for Conferences—Typically there are one or two sessions on Friday evening, and three or four sessions on Saturday, but there is flexibility: conferences can be spread over three days or kept to one day, and Q&A sessions can be added.

Outreach—Consider viewing the conference as an outreach to share Christ with your community. Pastor Scott can run a Facebook ad, and/or set up a Facebook event page for those in the church to share with others.

For more information, including sample messages and endorsements, please visit:

www.scottlapierre.org/conferences-and-speaking.

Marriage God's Way Workbook

The perfect companion to *Marriage God's Way*!

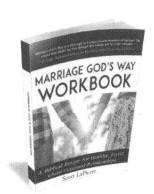

The workbook will help you apply the biblical recipe you learned in this book. It contains:

- Clear instructions on prayer, communication, and forgiveness
- Insightful questions that solve marital frustrations
- Practical exercises to enjoy with your spouse
- Important discussion topics that strengthen your relationship

Use this great tool in your marriage, small group, or church. It is perfect for engaged couples, newlyweds, and marriage veterans. There are questions for husbands, wives, and both as a couple:

- Husband: What are three ways your wife makes you feel respected? Disrespected?
- Wife: Second only to Christ, do you feel like the supreme relationship in your husband's life? Why or why not?
- Husband: When your wife is suffering, do you feel like she takes it out on you like Rachel did with Jacob (Genesis 30:1)?
- Wife: What can your husband do to help you more easily resist the temptation to nag him?
- Both: What do we have in our home that threatens our holiness, and how do we remove it?
- Regardless of the person asked, the purpose of each question is to help you have a *healthy, joyful, Christ-centered relationship*!

Enduring Trials God's Way:
A Biblical Recipe for Finding Joy in Suffering

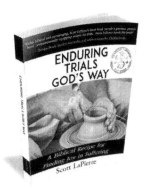

Trials are part of life on this side of heaven, and God wants to use them for your good! Pastor Scott LaPierre presents scriptural principles that give believers the encouragement they need when suffering. Every chapter concludes with questions that help you apply what you are reading. With *Enduring Trials God's Way* you will:

- Develop the spiritual perspective to embrace trials
- Appreciate the maturity trials produce
- Understand the rewards for enduring trials
- Recognize God is still compassionate and gracious during trials
- Learn to persevere through trials that threaten your faith

Endorsed by well-known ministry leaders:

- "Richly biblical and encouraging, Scott LaPierre's latest book reveals a gracious pastor's heart, compassionately equipping people for trials. Every believer needs this book!"

  —**Douglas Bond**—Speaker, tour leader, and author of twenty-five books of biography, practical theology, and historical fiction
- "One of the best biblical treatments of suffering I have seen. You want this book in your library!"

  —**Dr. Carlton McLeod**—Speaker, author, and senior pastor of Calvary Revival Church Chesapeake

A Father Offers His Son:
The True and Greater Sacrifice
Revealed Through Abraham and Isaac

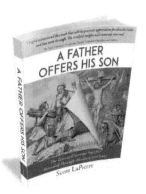

Have you ever wondered why God asked Abraham to sacrifice his son in Genesis 22? The Angel stopped Abraham showing God did not intend for him to kill Isaac, but what did God desire? God wanted to test Abraham, and readers will discover the account primarily reveals:

- In human terms what God would do with His Son two thousand years later
- The many ways Abraham and Isaac are a picture of God and His Son
- The tremendous love of God shown through Christ's sacrifice

Learn the remarkable parallels between God and Abraham, and Jesus and Isaac. With thought-provoking questions at the end of each chapter, the book is perfect for personal use or small groups.

A Father Offers His Son has been endorsed by well-known ministry leaders:

- **Dr. Paul Benware:** "I highly recommend this work that will deepen your appreciation for what the Father and Son went through. The excellent insights will encourage your soul."
  —Professor, Pastor, Speaker, and Author
- **Cary Green:** "As a jeweler holds a gemstone and examines each priceless, shining facet, Pastor Scott holds high this picture of heaven's sacrificial love and examines every detail."
  —Senior Pastor, Missionary, and Church

Made in the USA
San Bernardino, CA
28 November 2018